DO NOT
ALIGHT HERE

WALKING LONDON'S LOST
UNDERGROUND AND
RAILWAY STATIONS

Ben Pedroche

CAPITAL HISTORY

Acknowledgements
Many thanks to Louise Trueman for the support and the
wonderful photographs, to my family, to Nick Agnew and Peter
Nichols for reading the draft text and making helpful
suggestions, to Jim Connor for answering some queries, and to
Jim Whiting for the opportunity to write this book.

www.donotalighthere.com

ISBN 978 185414 352 5

First published 2011
Published by
Capital History
www.capitalhistory.com

Printed by 1010 Printing International Ltd

Contents

A few notes about using this book

As a wise man once said, the times they are a changin', and none more so than in a city like London; a place that's constantly rejuvenating itself to meet the demands of its people. The downside is that a few of the places listed in this book may have changed by the time you arrive to explore them. In particular, the areas behind St Pancras and Kings Cross stations are currently undergoing massive reconstruction, as is the area in and around Farringdon station. Also at time of writing, much of the route included in the walk from Canning Town to North Woolwich is about to be redeveloped as part of the mighty Crossrail project that will eventually transform London's rail infrastructure when it finally opens.

Where possible, the walks avoid long periods between locations where there isn't anything specific to see. However, on occasion the only logical route between one site to the next demands the odd 20 minute or so stretch before the next location. A few of the sites included also have no visible trace left of what was once there, but these are kept to a minimum and are only included when they fit logically into a planned route, or to add context to other parts of the walk.

Although each walk takes the quickest and easiest route from A to B, with clear directions and accurate listing of street names, London's complex system of streets and roads can sometimes be daunting, with the added problem that a few of the street names are not signposted (the book gives guidance where such instances occur).

Lastly, in addition to being a journey through London's forgotten rail and tube history, the book should also be seen as the chance to explore some of the cities' lesser-visited areas, even if the place in question is often considered off-limits. Although sometimes a little rough around the edges, many of London's less affluent areas can often be some of its most-vibrant, full of interesting characters and hidden gems.

Author's Introduction

Ever since trips down from the North with the family as a teenager, and later when I moved there full time, London has always been a place of great intrigue for me. A city heaving with people. The constant buzz of excitement. Hyper-modern yet bound by its long history. The place where there's always something happening. But amongst everything else, the thing about London that fascinates me the most is its wonderful transport network. Hundreds of buses running day and night, trains that weave through the streets to and from the suburbs, and of course, the magnificent Underground, burrowing its way through the subterranean depths. It's a system that works as the life blood of the city, pumping through its veins and arteries, keeping it flowing on an endless run of journeys from one great place to the next.

Something else that has always intrigued me is the idea of urban decay, in particular derelict and abandoned buildings, and the long-forgotten stories that lie behind them. And there's certainly no shortage of buildings that fall into this category on London's rail and tube network. From closed stations now faded from glory, to secret doorways, abandoned tunnels, strange bricked-up structures and so much more, you do not have to look too far to find traces of the city's hidden transport past.

It's these passions combined that have inspired me to write *Do Not Alight Here*. Inside you'll find a book of two parts. The first is a series of walks that take you on a journey through London's disused rail and Underground history, covering over 100 locations that span numerous boroughs in every direction. Then it's time to go underground for a look at the secrets of what can be seen when you peer through the tube window into the darkness, and a series of above-ground train journeys for a glimpse of various trackside station remains and more.

Exploring sites like the ones in this book can become addictive to say the least. After months spent walking around London researching this book, I now find myself assuming that every locked door I see in a tube station has to lead to some secret old passage, or that every boarded-up building must have at some point been an old railway station, although it usually turns out to be nothing more than wishful thinking. Now it's your turn to go and find out.

Explore and enjoy.

WALK 1

History and Progress: the ever-changing face of central London

This walk takes you through the heart of the capital, passing a huge selection of tourist attractions along the way. It covers some of the busiest areas of the city, meaning that the various abandoned stations, tram tunnels and bridges included are passed by millions of people every year, without ever being noticed. This makes it a genuine trip through secret London. Despite covering a relatively small area compared with other walks in the book; it's actually the longest in duration, proving just how frequently the most heavily-used part of a city can change so dramatically in the space of just a few years.

START: Holborn (Central and Piccadilly lines)

FINISH: Tower Hill (Circle and District lines, DLR from Tower Gateway)

TIME: 2 hours, 35 minutes

Exit Holborn station via the main exit on to Kingsway (or on to High Holborn if you decide to take the right exit). Next, turn right and cross over High Holborn on to Southampton Row (or cross High Holborn and turn left on to Southampton Row if you used the other exit). At the end of the street, where it meets the junction with Vernon Place on the left and Theobald's Road to the right, in the middle of the road lies one of the entrances to the **Kingsway Tramway Subway** tunnel.

Cross to the middle of the street at the traffic lights, and the abandoned entrance and downward ramp into the tunnel can clearly be seen. It was opened in 1906 and included stations

Tram Subway entrance at the top end of Kingsway, last used by trams in April 1952.

at Holborn (**Holborn Tramway Station**) and Aldwych (**Aldwych Tramway Station**). The tramline closed in 1952 and the tunnel became abandoned, although it did find a new use in the 1970s as an office for a flood control centre. It is now a Grade II listed structure and is used for storing road signs and other items of street furniture. The other end of the tunnel was lost when it was reconstructed as part of the Strand Underpass road tunnel.

Turn left on to Vernon Place and head straight, passing Bloomsbury Square Gardens and the point where the street now becomes Bloomsbury Way. Next, turn left on to New Oxford Street, in the direction back towards Holborn. Where the road name becomes High Holborn, the branch of Nationwide in the building on the corner of Bloomsbury Court marks the former location of **British Museum** tube station, opened in 1900 by the Central London Railway (CLR), the route of which today forms part of the Central line.

The station suffered competition from the Piccadilly line station at nearby Holborn, a problem later made even worse when the CLR opened its own set of Holborn platforms in 1933. Closure came in 1933, although the platforms below were used by the Army in the 1960s. The station building was demolished in 1989 and replaced by the commercial building seen today.

Trains still pass through the obvious remains of the platforms however, and these are included in the tube journey described later in the book from Tottenham Court Road to Whitechapel. Some claim the station to be haunted by the spirit of a disgruntled Egyptian mummy from the nearby museum after which the station is named. While the chances of this being true are slim to none, there is something genuinely eerie about what can be seen when trains pass through.

Continue along High Holborn, crossing back over Kingsway and Southampton Row, and the entrance to Holborn where the walk started. When you reach building number 31–33 on the left side of the street, known as Chancery Station House, this is one of the former entrances to the **Chancery Lane Deep Level Shelter**; the tube station of the same name being one of eight that had an additional set of tunnels built below their passenger platforms for use during World War II (see Walks 2 and 6 for the other London Underground stations with deep level shelters).

Chancery Lane station original entrance, later giving access to a World War II deep level shelter.

It was used as an air raid shelter during the war, and was later converted into the Kingsway Telephone Exchange of the General Post Office. The other entrance to the shelter was situated on a small side street named Took's Court, close to Furnival Street. This was demolished in 2002 however, with little now remaining to suggest it was ever there.

Continue along until you reach the actual entrance to Chancery Lane tube station, opened by the CLR in 1900. Now turn left on to Gray's Inn Road, crossing over the junction with Theobald's Road on the left and Clerkenwell Road to the right. Just after, turn right on to a small side street named Mount Pleasant. Follow to the end, and then bear right when the street opens up to a much wider size.

Mail Rail entrance at Mount Pleasant sorting office.

Next, turn left on to Phoenix Place, and the huge complex of buildings along the right is Royal Mail's Mount Pleasant Sorting Office. When the road bears towards the right, you'll see a disused gate with a faded sign listing this as being the entrance to the **Post Office Railway,** branded more recently as Mail Rail. It was a private underground rail network operated by Royal Mail, with specially-designed, unmanned trains sending mail across the city. It was opened by the General Post Office in 1927 and the route ran from Paddington Sorting Office to Whitechapel Eastern Delivery Office, with seven stops along the way, including Mount Pleasant. It was closed permanently in 2003 after it proved to be far less economical than using road vehicles.

Turn right at the end of Phoenix Place on to Calthorpe Street, keeping the sorting office on your right. Turn right at the end, on to Farringdon Road, and keep straight on. As you head towards the junction with Clerkenwell Road, the brick wall along the left side of the street hides tracks in a cutting down below on the approach to Farringdon station. Turn left on to Clerkenwell Road and cross over where the road bridges the tracks below, pausing briefly to glance at the great view of St Paul's Cathedral to the right.

Turn right on to Turnmill Street soon after (not signposted), and further along the right side of the road you'll find Farringdon station, undergoing massive renovation work at the time of writing. It opened in 1863, making it one of the oldest tube stations on the network, and much of the original building is still in use. This can be seen in all its glory from the corner of Turnmill Street and Cowcross Street, complete with its 1922 name of Farringdon and High Holborn in the stonework along the top. This is in fact however a replacement of an even earlier long-demolished station building that originally opened as Farringdon Street.

Turn right on to Cowcross Street itself, past the station entrance and then left at the end, back on to Farringdon Road. The sad and mostly derelict remains of Smithfield Market can be seen along the left, and the Holborn Viaduct road bridge can be seen up ahead. But just before you reach it, turn left instead on to Snow Hill, and the derelict and dirty-looking building along the left is the location of the former **Snow Hill** station.

It was opened in 1874 by the London, Chatham and Dover Railway (LC&DR) as an additional set of platforms to serve Holborn Viaduct station further ahead. Its name was later changed to Holborn Viaduct Low Level, but by 1916 the station had closed its doors for good. Snow Hill's platforms were located below, inside the Snow Hill Tunnel, built by the LC&DR in 1866. It closed at the same time as the station in

1916, although was still used by freight trains until the 1960s. It then sat disused for years until being brought back into service in 1989 as part of the Thameslink network. Although the station building is long gone, it is believed that the black door mid-way along the derelict building is an emergency exit that leads down to the abandoned platforms, traces of which can be seen from passing trains (see the train journey from West Hampstead Thameslink to Herne Hill later in the book).

Continue along, where the road bears right and ends at the junction with Holborn Viaduct. The office building known as Fleet Place House directly ahead marks the location of **Holborn Viaduct** station itself, opened in 1874 by the LC&DR. It closed in 1990 after years of service reductions, and was finally demolished a few years later. Although nothing remains of the old station, part of its former site is now home to City Thameslink station, opened in 1990 under the original name of St Paul's Thameslink. Head right, towards the Holborn Viaduct road bridge, for great views of the Fleet Valley, where the River Fleet once ran through the streets of London from Hampstead Heath to here on its way towards the Thames. It's now buried and redirected below ground, making it the city's longest subterranean river.

Door leading to disused Snow Hill platforms

Disused Aldwych station entrance opened as Strand station in 1907

Walk down the grand set of steps on the left side of Holborn Viaduct, down to Farringdon Road below, although by this point it is now called Farringdon Street. After a few minutes you'll arrive at Ludgate Circus, where the entrance to City Thameslink on Ludgate Hill, to the left, is the former location of **Ludgate Hill** station. Another stop on the LC&DR, it was opened in 1865 but suffered from low passenger numbers and eventually closed in 1929. Its platforms were located up above, on a long-since demolished viaduct that crossed over the road between what is now Waterstones and a branch of Santander bank.

Now turn right on to Fleet Street, famous for being synonymous with the newspaper industry and Sweeney Todd. Bear left just after the Royal Courts of Justice, then, after the road now becomes the Strand, turn left on to Surrey Street. On the right side of the street you'll find the easy-to-spot and well preserved **Aldwych** tube station building, opened under the name Strand in 1907 by the Brompton and Piccadilly Circus Railway (the Piccadilly line).

The station was at the end of a short branch line that connected with the rest of the line at Holborn, and had its name changed to Aldwych in 1915. The branch was closed in 1994 after low usage made necessary upgrade work hard to justify, but the station has proven to be lucrative since closure, often being hired by film and TV production companies looking to film scenes on the Underground network.

Retrace your steps back to the Strand and turn left, and just after the corner of Surrey Street you'll find another former entrance to the station, with its original name still displayed. Continue straight, passing Somerset House on the left, and then turn left on to Lancaster Place. Head over the River Thames along Waterloo Bridge, and when you reach the other side, take either of the subway ramps on each side of the road, following signs for Waterloo station (all routes lead to the station, making the prospect of missing it from here almost impossible).

When you get to Waterloo, enter the station via its grand entrance on Station Approach. It has been one of London's greatest termini ever since it was opened as Waterloo Bridge Station by the London and South Western Railway (L&SWR) in 1848. It has its own disused section, but surprisingly, this is the result of a more recent change. Just after you enter the station, the area to the right of the current platforms is the abandoned **Waterloo International** part of the station. Home to Eurostar trains when the service was launched in 1994, the station lasted less than 15 years when it was closed as a result of Eurostar moving its operation to St Pancras International in 2007.

Exit the station via the small side entrance and looking left from here reveals just how big the abandoned section is. It has been used in recent years for theatre productions of *The Railway Children*, including a steam train located on one of the disused tracks. For the most part however, the station sits empty, proving to have been a huge waste of time and money.

Restored former entrance to Blackfriars Road station.

Head back through the station and out the same way you entered. Cross Station Approach and head right on to Mepham Street, then right again at the end, on to Waterloo Road. When you reach the entrance to Waterloo tube station, turn left on to The Cut. Next, turn left again when you reach Southwark tube station, this time on to Blackfriars Road. Under the rail bridge can be found the old entrances to **Blackfriars Road** station, opened in 1864 by the South Eastern Railway. It closed in 1868 after becoming redundant thanks to the opening of nearby Waterloo Junction station, later renamed Waterloo East. One of the former entrances is now home to a newsagent, but the restored frontage proudly displays the station name.

Remains of Blackfriars Bridge station, closed in 1885.

Continue along Blackfriars Road until you reach the junction with Southwark Street. A narrow side street on the right called Invicta Plaza is where you can see the scant remains of **Blackfriars Bridge** station. It was opened by the LC&DR in 1864, serving as the terminus of their line from south London until it was extended over the Thames later in the year.

The opening of a bigger Blackfriars station on the other side of the river led to the closure of Blackfriars Bridge station in 1885, after which the site was converted into a goods yard. This closed in 1964 and most of the complex was demolished in the 1960s. The area opposite Invicta Plaza, now home to Bar 242, is where the bulk of the goods yard complex was located, although most of this has also now disappeared.

Keep walking along Blackfriars Road, and just before the road continues over the river, looking to the right allows you to see Blackfriars Railway Bridge and the station built on top. This is the second bridge here, serving as a replacement to the original built by the LC&DR in 1864. This was dismantled in 1985 after the new station opened, leaving the bridge abutments to rust away, marooned in the middle of the river along with an ornate LC&DR crest. The abutments were nevertheless brought back into action in 2011 as part of an ambitious project to expand the platforms at Blackfriars station.

Retrace your steps back towards the old station site and this time turn left on to Southwark Street, looking out for bricked-up doorways under the bridge that reveal more evidence of the closed station above. Turn left after the bridge and on to Hopton Street, then bear right when you reach Falcon Point Plaza. The old Bankside Power Station building is now directly ahead, now better known as the home of the Tate Modern. Walk towards it and then turn left towards the river.

Head right, admiring the spectacular view of the Millennium Bridge, St Paul's and the City. Follow the path when it heads under the subway below Southwark Bridge, after which you can see **Cannon Street** station on the other side of the river. It was opened by the South Eastern Railway in 1866, and although still in use today, it was originally built on a far grander scale. Most of the original building was demolished in the late 1950s, leaving only the two tall brickwork towers that can be seen from here. Continue along the path until you reach the Anchor Pub, at which point the path heads away from the river and passes under the Cannon Street Railway Bridge. Follow the narrow streets and pathways, passing various highlights including the Clink Prison, the remains of Winchester Palace and the replica of the Golden Hinde. Bear left and head around Southwark Cathedral before then passing under another bridge just beyond the Mudlark pub. Shortly after, the road brings you out on to Tooley Street, with London Bridge station directly ahead.

Turn right and head straight, keeping the station on your left. The road now changes to being called Duke Street Hill, and when you reach the end, turn left on to Borough High Street. Just after walking under the bridge, turn left again, and on the corner of Railway Approach you can find a disused London Bridge station entrance. It formed part of the original station built in 1900 by the City & South London Railway (C&SLR), but closed when the entire station complex was rebuilt below ground in 1967.

Retrace your steps back to the corner of Borough High Street and Duke Street Hill, but this time continue straight and head over the bridge back across the Thames. When you reach the other side, the name of the road is now King William Street, and the office building on the right named Regis House marks the former location of **King William Street** station.

Plaque on the side of Regis House, former location of King William Street station.

Second site of closed Mark Lane Underground station.

It was opened by the C&SLR in 1890 and closed a decade later in 1900. The station building was demolished in the 1930s, but a blue commemorative plaque on the side of Regis House on Monument Street pays tribute to its history. The platforms below still exist and were used as an air raid shelter in World War II. Trains still pass the tunnels that lead from the main line to King William Street, and these are included in the tube journey from Stockwell to Golders Green/Kentish Town.

Turn right on to Monument Street towards the Monument itself (built in honour of the Great Fire that started in nearby Pudding Lane), right again on to the wonderfully named Fish Street Hill, then left on to Lower Thames Street. Bear left uphill where the road becomes Byward Street. Shortly after the road bears right, the branch of All Bar One on the corner of Seething Lane is the former location of **Mark Lane** tube station.

The area was originally served by a station known as **Tower of London** that was opened in 1882 by the Metropolitan Railway (MR), and closed just two years later in 1884. It was replaced later in the same year by Mark Lane station, which served MR and also Metropolitan District Railway (MDR) trains. The two companies worked in conjunction to run the Inner Circle line; the predecessor of today's Circle line.

The original Mark Lane station building on the corner was demolished in 1911 and replaced by a simple entrance further along the street, now used as the entrance to a pedestrian subway. The subway itself has been constructed inside what used to be a footbridge that connected the two platforms, and the noise of trains passing below can be heard through the metal grills. Some remains of the platforms below can still be seen. The station closed in 1967 after its success began to exceed capacity, with minimal scope for expansion. It was replaced by a new Tower Hill station nearby (Mark Lane had itself changed name to Tower Hill in 1946).

Walk through the subway and turn left when you emerge on the other side of the road. Head for the Tower of London and turn right when you reach the ticket office. Just after the ticket office and the row of food stalls on the right side you'll find a cylindrical concrete structure. This is one of the entrances to the **Tower Subway**, built in 1868, and technically the first-ever underground train tunnel. Passengers were carried through the tunnel and under the river inside small cable-operated pods. It proved to be a failure however, and the tunnel was instead converted for pedestrian use. Closure came in 1898 and it is now used to carry water mains.

Retrace your steps back to Byward Street and now head right. A subway under the road further ahead leads you to the current Tower Hill station, where the walk ends. The station is on the Circle and District line, and is also a short walk to Tower Gateway Docklands Light Railway (DLR) station.

Tower Subway entrance shaft, next to the Tower of London.

WALK 2

Camden Borough Part 1: walking the great London termini

This journey starts by taking a look at a little piece of military history that lies right in the heart of central London. The route then heads north towards three of the city's most important railway termini, all of which lie close together in the vast London Borough of Camden. Each station has changed many times over the years, leaving relics along the way that can still be spotted amongst the ambitious urban regeneration projects that are currently reshaping the area once again.

START: Goodge Street (Northern line)

FINISH: Kings Cross station (National Rail) or Kings Cross St Pancras (Circle, Hammersmith & City, Metropolitan, Northern, Piccadilly and Victoria lines)

TIME: 50 minutes

Exit Goodge Street tube station on to Tottenham Court Road. Head right, then turn left on to Chenies Street. On the left side of the road you'll find a strange looking building known as the Eisenhower Centre. This is the east entrance to the **Goodge Street Deep Level Shelter**, one of a series of extra tunnels built under the platforms of eight tube stations in the run up to World War II (see Walk 6 for more on the history of the shelters). While some were later used by the public as air raid shelters, the one at Goodge Street was used by the Supreme Headquarters Allied Expeditionary Force (SHAEF), commanded by Dwight Eisenhower. It fell into disuse after the war ended, and has since been converted into an archive and data storage facility. Continue along, and next turn left down Huntley Street, then left again on to Torrington Place. When you reach the end, at the junction back on to Tottenham Court Road, directly opposite is the west entrance to the shelter.

Goodge Street deep level shelter building, now the Eisenhower Centre and used for secure storage.

West entrance to the shelter at Goodge Street.

Head back down Torrington Place and keep straight until you reach Gower Street, at which point turn left. At the end, turn right on to Euston Road, passing the entrance to Euston Square tube station. Cross over to the other side of the road when you reach the corner of Gordon Street, and head straight on to Melton Street.

On the right you'll find a green area that leads to Euston station, one of London's key main line termini ever since it was opened by the London and Birmingham Railway (L&BR) in 1837. It's a station that has seen much redevelopment over the decades, and perhaps none more so than when it became part of the Underground network in 1907. The first set of tube platforms were opened here by the City & South London Railway (C&SLR). This was followed by another set later in the same year opened by their competitors, the Charing Cross, Euston & Hampstead Railway (CCE&HR).

Both sets of platforms had their own entrance buildings until these were closed in 1914 and replaced with the entrance inside the Network Rail station that is still used today. The two separate tube companies were later merged to form what is now the Northern Line. The C&SLR building is long gone, but the CCE&HR entrance is still intact and can be seen by heading up Melton Street. It's on the corner of Drummond Street and is instantly recognisable as having the ox-blood tiling that was a common feature of tube stations designed by Leslie Green (see Walk 4 for more). It is now used as a sub-station and ventilation shaft from the station below. A vast network of disused corridors that once linked the two separate sets of platforms also still exists, locked away from the eyes of the public.

Head back down Melton Street and turn left back on to Euston Road. As you pass the station on the left, the point in the middle where buses turn in to stop at the station forecourt is roughly the location of the **Euston Arch** (also commonly referred to as the Doric Arch), a huge stone archway that stood at the front of the station. It was built as part of the original complex in 1837 but was controversially demolished in the 1960s, despite much protest.

Keep walking along and after a few minutes you will reach the corner of Ossulston Street. The great stations of St Pancras and Kings Cross lie just ahead, but first you'll find the British

Library, which itself is built on the site of the former **Somers Town goods yard**. It opened in 1877 as part of St Pancras's own goods facility, and specialised in the movement of potatoes. Closure and demolition came in the 1970s, followed by replacement with the library in 1997.

Walk along Ossulston Street, where fragments of the yard's brick wall can still be seen along the right, as well as an open area of land now used as a car park. Turn right on to Brill Lane for further remains, including an entrance gate (everything listed here was clearly visible at the time of writing, but the entire site was about to be redeveloped and turned into a new facility for the UK Centre for Medical Research and Innovation).

Turn right at the end of Brill Lane on to Midland Road, then left at the end, back on to Euston Road. From here you can now see St Pancras station on the left in all its magnificent beauty. It was opened in 1868 by the Midland Railway as the terminus of their new Midland Main Line. It was redeveloped in 2007 and renamed St Pancras International, to celebrate the opening of the Eurostar platforms. The work included refurbishment of the awe-inspiring train shed roof, originally engineered by William Henry Barlow. Although hard to imagine now, the station was earmarked for closure and demolition in the 1960s. The decision was reversed after a massive campaign against the plans, championed by Sir John Betjeman. The efforts of the great Poet Laureate have now been immortalised by a statue that stands proudly in the station.

The lavish building seen from the Euston Road that sits above the station is the former **Midland Grand Hotel**, built in 1865 before the station below had even opened. It was closed in 1935, and was later used as offices by British Rail under the name St Pancras Chambers. It lay dormant for years, until finally being reopened in 2011 as the St Pancras Renaissance London Hotel.

Original Somers Town goods yard wall, located behind the British Library.

Turn left just after the building, on to Pancras Road, keeping the station to your left. On the right from here can be seen the main train shed building of Kings Cross station, looking much the same as it did when it was opened by the Great Northern Railway (GNR) in 1852. A little further after passing the side entrance to St Pancras, turn right on to Goods Way. The derelict and dirty looking building to the left as you walk up the slight hill is the Great Northern Railway Coal & Fish Offices. It was part of **Kings Cross goods yard**, which was opened at a similar time as the station, and included facilities for moving goods to and from barges on the Regent's Canal.

The well preserved but disused York Road tube station.

As you walk further along Goods Way, the view from both sides of the road reveals the true scale of the huge development Kings Cross Central. Turn left at the end on to York Way. After you cross over the canal, the various derelict buildings and train sheds on the left are the rest of what remains of the goods yard, which closed in 1973. Continue along, and after a few minutes, on the right side of the road you'll arrive at the disused **York Road** tube station, located on the corner of the tiny, un-signposted Bingfield Street. It's easily recognized as another Leslie Green building, and the words 'York Road Station' can still clearly be seen on the front.

It was opened in 1906 as a stop on the Great Northern, Piccadilly & Brompton Railway (GNP&BR), much of which became what is now the Piccadilly line (see Walk 4 for more closed stations on this route). Even from the start it failed to attract much custom and it was closed for good in 1932. It's interesting to note that its closure explains why there is such a long gap between Kings Cross St Pancras and Caledonian Road when you travel along the Piccadilly line. The remains of the station's platforms can still be seen from passing trains, and these are included in the tube journey from Gloucester Road to Arsenal described later in the book.

Continue along York Way, passing under a rail bridge further ahead. Just after walking under the next bridge, look upwards on the left side of the road, and on the side of the bridge you'll see a bricked-up doorway. This is all that remains of one of the two **Maiden Lane** stations that were located here. The first was opened in 1850 by the GNR, and operated for just two years as the temporary terminus of the line until Kings Cross was completed in 1852.

The other station was opened in the same year by the East & West India Docks & Birmingham Junction Railway, which later became the North London Railway (NLR). It closed in 1917, but still operated as a goods yard that worked in conjunction with the Kings Cross yard. Although the GNR station is long demolished, traces of the later station still remain, as evidenced by the doorway marooned up high with nowhere to go.

Now retrace your steps all the way back down York Way, passing Goods Way and continuing on towards Kings Cross, ensuring you are on the right side of the road. When you reach the point just before where the station building begins, you'll see a gap in the brick wall along the right side of the road, parallel to the entrance to Wharfdale Road. This is the former entrance to **Kings Cross York Road**, an auxiliary station of the main one, opened in 1862 for GNR suburban services. It

Former location of the platforms at Kings Cross York Road main line station.

closed in 1976, but a few remains can still be seen. The ramp located through the gap in the wall was how passengers would have reached the platforms. These were situated in the area seen towards the right, still used by trains running in and out of the main station.

When you reach the end of York Way, turn left away from the station and on to Pentonville Road. Next, turn right on to Kings Cross Bridge, a short but busy stretch of road with the Scala music venue on the left and a row of shops on the right. Between the shops you'll find a grimy looking doorway with signage that hints at having something to do with the London Underground. It is used today as a fire exit and access for engineers, but is actually one of the old entrances to a different Kings Cross station, opened by the Metropolitan Railway in 1863.

All that remains of the original Kings Cross Metropolitan line station building, looking as though it could do with a bit of a clean.

Given the official name **Kings Cross Metropolitan** in order to differentiate from the larger GNR station, it had four platforms and was built in a cutting. The station was served by one of the company's own early tube lines, most of which now forms the Metropolitan line. The other two platforms were used by the Great Western Railway (GWR). Their original station entrance was on Gray's Inn Road, but this is long since demolished.

Turn left at the end of Kings Cross Bridge, briefly on to Gray's Inn Road and then left again down a tiny alleyway known as St Chad's Place. Look through the railings on the left hand side and you'll see down into what remains of a platform that was part of the old Metropolitan side of the station, which closed in 1940 when it was replaced by the station used today that connects the modernised Kings Cross with St Pancras. Metropolitan line trains still run through the old platforms seen below, and are included in the Underground journey from Finchley Road to Liverpool Street later in the book.

The main line side of the station is now hidden behind the wall to the right of the old Met platform. This had also closed by 1979, but was then reopened in 1983 with the new name Kings Cross Midland City. The name was changed again to **Kings Cross Thameslink** in 1988 when the line became part of the Thameslink route. These platforms themselves closed in 2007 when the route switched to a new set of platforms built as part of the redeveloped St Pancras International station. First Capital Connect trains still run through the abandoned platforms however, and are included in the train journey later on from West Hampstead Thameslink to Herne Hill. Peer over the walls further along the alleyway on the right and you may catch a glimpse of the top of an old platform canopy.

Continue along St Chad's Place until it narrows, turns sharply to the left and then goes along a short tunnel under the buildings above. This brings you out on to Kings Cross Road, at which point turn left, then bear left again back on to Pentonville Road. Further along you'll find a side entrance to Kings Cross St Pancras Underground, only open at certain times. This is the former entrance to the Thameslink station, which itself replaced an earlier entrance to the original 1863 station. Continue straight and after a few minutes you will arrive back at Kings Cross station, where the walk ends.

Kings Cross includes rail services to various London suburbs and further afield to Peterborough, Cambridge, Leeds, York and more. It's also served by six different tube lines. The walk can also be ended further along at St Pancras, whose services include Thameslink trains from Bedford to Brighton, Midland Main Line routes to the East Midlands and Sheffield, and international lines to France and Belgium.

WALK 3

Camden Borough Part 2: Midlands to the Metropolis

The walk that follows is a journey across the north London borough of Camden. The route looks at what remains of ambitious plans by many different rail companies of the mid-late 1800s, at a time when they were in fierce competition to create the fastest routes into London from the North. Although lots of stations have since disappeared, all of these pioneering lines are still used today, a testament to the foresight of the designers and engineers that made them a reality.

START: Finchley Road (Metropolitan and Jubilee lines)

FINISH: Camden Town (Northern line)

TIME: 2 hours

Exit Finchley Road station and turn left onto Finchley Road itself, passing the various shops and restaurants. Just after the O2 Centre, cross the small road at the traffic lights ahead, and stop where the road bridges the train tracks seen to the left down below. The area just beyond the bridge, currently covered by fencing and billboards, is the site of the demolished **Finchley Road** railway station. It opened in 1868 with the longer name of Finchley Road & St John's Wood, built by the Midland Railway as part of an extension to their existing line from the North, which until then had terminated at Bedford. This now gave the company a direct route into St Pancras, instead of having to defer passengers to rival services if they wanted to continue into central London when they reached Bedford. The station complex also included a goods yard, and the tracks were used for a short time by trains on the Super Outer Circle; an unsuccessful venture by the Midland Railway that used a combination of rail and Underground lines to form a fast service for the suburbs.

Brickwork remains of Finchley Road railway station.

Like many other stations at the time, Finchley Road fell victim to low passenger numbers and eventually closed in 1927. Although the station building has completely gone, remnants of brickwork still remain, including traces of the steps that would have led to the platforms. These can be seen by peering over the concrete wall of the bridge itself (not actually a bridge at all. What lies below is in fact the entrance to the Belsize Tunnels, through which trains would have entered immediately after leaving the station), and by walking down the slip road next to the O2 Centre (Blackburn Road, although it's not signposted). The tracks are today used by services along the Midland Main Line, operated by First Capital Connect and East Midland Trains, and these are included in the train journey later in the book from West Hampstead Thameslink to Herne Hill.

Retrace your steps back to Finchley Road Underground station, but this time turn right just after the entrance, onto Canfield Gardens. Head straight, and then turn left when you reach Priory Road, a typical north London street of eye-wateringly expensive houses. Cross over Abbey Road (the famous studio and Beatles zebra crossing is roughly 15 minutes walk to the left) and continue along the remainder of Priory Road until it meets Belsize Road, at which point turn right. Cross over to the left hand side, and where the road bends to the left just after a row of shops, the building now used as a second-hand furniture store is a disused section of **Kilburn High Road** station. Continue along, keeping the brick wall and billboards on your left, behind which are the station's current platforms. As the pavement starts to go up hill, the back of what was once the original station building can be seen over the wall, now used as commercial premises. When you reach the end, turn left onto the vibrant Kilburn High Road.

The hairdressers and kebab shop on the corner mark where the original station entrance once stood, and if you look above them, there are faint traces of what looks to be an original station sign. It was opened by the London and North Western Railway (L&NWR) in 1852 under the name Kilburn & Maida Vale, on a route that now forms part of the West Coast Main Line (WCML). The entrance to the station of today can be found further along, now part of London Overground.

Although the station now only has two platforms, there were originally four, the other two having been taken out of service and demolished when the layout was reconfigured to allow fast services to pass through the station at high speed without stopping, although some fragments may still be seen through the wooden fence along Platform 2. Other traces of the station's larger scale can be seen by walking the length of both platforms, including the opposite side of the furniture shop building seen earlier. More can be seen from passing trains, and the station is included in the rail journey from Clapham Junction to Euston later in the book.

Abandoned and overgrown platforms at South Hampstead.

Continue on past the station and turn left when you reach Greville Road just after the Kilburn Library Centre. Then turn left again on to Kilburn Priory, and just before you rejoin Belsize Road, look over the left wall when the road bridges the tracks below for a birds-eye view of the station and its disused parts.

Turn right, back on to Belsize Road, and head straight, crossing Abbey Road for a second time. After a few minutes, turn right onto Loudoun Road, and on the left you'll find the uninspiring entrance to **South Hampstead** station. Originally another stop on the L&NWR route, opened in 1879 with the name Loudoun Road, its present name dates from 1922.

Later reconstructed in the same way as Kilburn High Road to allow through-services, the two disused platforms have only been partially demolished, and their remains can clearly be seen by looking down over the wall and fence just after the station entrance, including a series of arched doorways in the brick wall along the right.

You can see this and more in even closer detail by entering the station and walking along both platforms. The station is also included in the Clapham Junction to Euston train journey later on, giving you the chance to see even more from track level. The original station building is long gone without a trace, replaced in the 1960's with the version seen today. The tunnels seen at the end of the platforms are the west portals of the Primrose Hill Tunnel, but more on that later.

Continue past the station entrance, then turn left onto Alexandra Road. Bear left, and then turn right onto Hillgrove Road, up the hill, then right again at the busy junction with Finchley Road. Cross over to the left side of the road and head straight, until you reach the corner of Queens Grove. The grand building on the corner is the closed **Marlborough Road** tube station, opened in 1868 as part of a new line created by the Metropolitan & Saint John's Wood Railway. Owned by the Metropolitan Railway (MR), the new route was an extension of the company's expanding network, connecting Baker Street to a terminus at another new station further north at Swiss Cottage. The route today forms part of the Metropolitan line, and its trains still run through the station's abandoned platforms below.

By the 1930s the station was in decline, hit hard by competition from buses. The final nail in the coffin came when a new set of tunnels was built that provided a faster route from Baker Street, which included the opening of a new station at St John's Wood close by. The new tunnels were opened on the Bakerloo line and ran to Stanmore, until the route was later made part of what is now the Jubilee line.

It all proved too much for Marlborough Road and it closed in 1939, along with a similar station at **Lords** (opened in 1868 under the original name St John's Wood Road) and the station at **Swiss Cottage**. Although the other two station buildings have long since been demolished, Marlborough Road remains almost perfectly intact, at least from the outside.

Station building at Marlborough Road, closed in 1939.

The building was home to several restaurants in the decades that followed its closure, with the last one shutting its doors for good in early 2009. At time of writing, the station is being converted by Transport for London into a substation for the network. Stepping up onto the edge of the flower bed at the back of the station on the Finchley Road side allows you to see through the fence and down to where trains still pass by. Evidence of platform entrances and stairways can clearly be made out, and these are covered in more detail as part of the Finchley Road to Liverpool Street tube journey later in the book. In case you are wondering, the station was named after the street on the other side of Finchley Road, although its name has since been changed to Marlborough Place.

Return back down Finchley Road in the direction you came from, crossing back over to the left side of the road. Continue straight, passing the Odeon cinema and Ye Olde Swiss Cottage pub to the right. Just after passing Barclays Bank on the left, you'll see a London Underground sign that marks one of the entrances to the Jubilee line's Swiss Cottage tube station. To the right of this is a brick wall which covers a large vent above the disused Metropolitan sub-surface platforms of the original Swiss Cottage station.

Although nothing now remains, the station building itself stood a little further ahead. Opened in 1868 as the terminus of the new route from Baker Street, the original building looked similar to the one at Marlborough Road, but this itself was replaced by a more elegant building in the 1920s, including a parade of shops and accommodation. There was also a second entrance on Belsize Road, but the whole complex was demolished in the 1960s. Before closure in 1940, there was an interchange built between the station and its new replacement below ground on the Bakerloo line (now part of the Jubilee line), but it wasn't to last. Parts of the old platforms below can still be seen from passing trains, and these are included in the tube journey later.

Cross over Finchley Road itself and head right, onto Avenue Road, then left at the busy junction onto Adelaide Road, named after Queen Adelaide; wife of William IV. Continue straight for roughly ten minutes until you reach the junction with Primrose Hill Road. Turn right, and cross over to the left side of the road. In the 1800s, much of this area was owned by Eton College (reflected in the nearby streets names of Eton Avenue, Eton Road and Eton College Road), who objected to plans by the London and Birmingham Railway (L&BR) to open new lines through the area.

The railway eventually managed to convince the landowners to allow them access, but there was a condition that the affluent Chalcots Estate had to be crossed via a tunnel, with

Primrose Hill disused platforms with The Roundhouse in the distance.

the further caveat that its portals should be luxuriously designed. The result was the Primrose Hill Tunnel, and as you walk along Primrose Hill Road you are walking on top of it. It was London's first rail tunnel and a great feat of engineering that attracted attention from across the city when it was completed in 1838. A later set of portals were added in 1879, and the full set of east portals is now a Grade II listed structure. Turn left onto King Henry's Road, and the gaps through the fence on the left give you the chance to see the portals in all their magnificence, although they are now sadly overgrown and in a sorry state. A better view would have been available just a few yards ahead, but it's obscured by a National Grid sub-station.

Continue along King Henry's Road, and then turn left onto the pathway that forms a bridge over the tracks below. This is Bridge Approach, and the building at the far end on the right, currently a shop, is the former **Primrose Hill** station. It opened in 1855 with the name Hampstead Road, later changed to Chalk Farm, before changing again to Primrose Hill in 1950.

The station originally had two sets of platforms. One set served what is now the West Coast Main Line, but these were taken out of service in 1915. The other platforms formed part of the North London Railway (NLR), originally known by the less catchy name of the East & West India Docks & Birmingham Junction Railway. The route later formed part of the North London Line, which today still runs through the disused station site (covered in the Clapham Junction to Euston train journey). Closure came in 1992, but there are still obvious traces of its abandoned platforms, much of which can be seen by looking over the side of the bridge just before you reach the station.

Follow Bridge Approach to the end, and then turn right, back onto Adelaide Road. Now turn right onto Chalk Farm Road, just after you pass Chalk Farm tube station. A minute or so along, the round brick building on the right is the famous Roundhouse. It's a Grade II listed building that was built in 1846 by the London & Birmingham Railway as an engine shed complete with its own turntable. It's been used for gigs since the mid-1960s, playing host over the years to Pink Floyd, The Doors and Jimi Hendrix amongst many others. Further along on the same side of the road you'll find the entrance to Stables Market. Before being turned into one of the most popular attractions that the eccentric streets of Camden has to offer, the yard was home to the Midland Railway Stables & Horse Hospital, where horses that were used to pull the company's canal barges came to be treated for injury.

Turn left away from the busyness of Chalk Farm Road on to Hartland Road. Keep straight, passing under the rail bridge above, and then turn left on to Lewis Street, right on to Hadley Street, then right again on to Castle Road. Follow Castle Road to the end, where it now meets Kentish Town Road. Turn right, and almost immediately on the right you'll find a red-tiled building that used to be **South Kentish Town** tube station, now home to Cash Converters on the ground floor and a sauna above.

Closed South Kentish Town station, now used as commercial premises.

The station opened in 1907 as part of a line from Charing Cross to Archway, built by the Charing Cross, Euston & Hampstead Railway, although most people referred to the line by its nickname 'Hampstead Tube'. The CCE&HR was one of two lines that later merged to form today's Northern line (the other being the City and South London Railway).

Yet another victim of too few passengers, the station closed in 1924, but was later used as an air raid shelter during World War II. The building is another fine example of Leslie Green's work (see Walk 4), and it's perhaps best appreciated from the other side of the road. Although now sadly gated, the alleyway known as Castle Place allows you to see more of the building, including what would have been the side entrance. The remains of the platforms below can easily be seen from passing trains, and these are included in the tube journey from Stockwell to Golders Green/Kentish Town.

Retrace your steps back to the corner of Castle Road, but this time continue along Kentish Town Road and then turn right onto Bartholomew Road, just after the church. Head straight, then bear right (ignoring where Bartholomew Villas runs off to the left). Turn left at the end where the street bends at a sharp corner next to Camden School for Girls. After a minute or so, turn right onto Oseney Crescent, after the van hire yard.

On the right you'll find the entrance to a park called Cantelowes Gardens. Head into the park, and by looking over the wall and through the metal fence on the right, you can see right down into the cutting that used to be the location of the **Camden Road** station platforms. Although virtually all traces of the platforms have now gone, gaps between the existing tracks hint that something used to be there. Midland Mainline and Thameslink trains pass through the site today just before disappearing back into the Camden Road Tunnels, and the route is included in the train journey from West Hampstead Thameslink to Herne Hill, covered later.

Now continue through the park along the path, keeping the skate park on your left, and out via the other gate onto Camden Road. Turn right, and the German car specialist garage on the right marks the spot where the station building used to be. Opened in 1868 by the Midland Railway as another stop on their new line into London, it was unpopular from the start and closed in 1916. The station building was demolished in the 1960s, although there appears to be a few tiny fragments remaining on Sandall Road.

Continue along Camden Road and after a few minutes you'll reach the current Camden Road station (London Overground), which itself appears to have disused doorways under the rail bridge above. It was opened in 1870 as Camden Town, a name that is still written as such in the stone work of the building high above the entrance. Continue straight until Camden Road comes to an end at the junction of Kentish Town Road and Camden High Street. This is also where you'll find Camden Town tube station, one of eight London Underground stations that had an additional deep-level tunnel built under its existing platforms in the early 1940s (see Walk 6).

Turn left onto Camden High Street, then right, into an alleyway called Underhill Passage. At the end of the alley, where it widens to become Underhill Street, look to the right for a strange looking brick building, which can be seen at the

Camden Town deep level shelter entrance, hidden away behind shops.

back of the small Marks & Spencer car park. This is one of the two entrance shafts to the actual **Camden Town Deep Level Shelter**. Unless the gates are locked, the building can be seen from even closer by walking along the slip road that runs along the side of the car park.

Retrace your steps back to Camden High Street and turn left, back towards the tube station. Continue straight, before then turning right onto Buck Street, located just after Camden Market. The street isn't signposted, but is easily identified by the Bucks Head pub on the corner. At the back of the market on the right, you'll find the other entrance shaft to the deep-level shelter, similar in style to the structure at the other end. Head back to Camden Town tube station where the walk ends. The station is on the Northern line, and gives you the option to head into central London via either the Bank or Charing Cross branch.

WALK 4

High Life and Low Passengers: Affluent Piccadilly and west London

This walks covers some of London's wealthiest districts, beginning in the centre at Piccadilly and ending in Chelsea, taking in Knightsbridge and Kensington along the way. The first part of the journey follows the route of the modern day Piccadilly line, passing a number of its original stations that have since closed. The walk then heads west, turning its attention to what remains of an ill-fated branch line that once served much of the Royal Borough of Kensington and Chelsea, yet suffered from low passenger numbers almost from the very start.

START: Green Park (Piccadilly, Victoria and Jubilee lines)

FINISH: West Brompton (District line, National Rail)

TIME: 2 hours

Start at Green Park tube station, leaving via the exit sign-posted as 'Piccadilly north side' (ignore the other close by exit listed as 'Piccadilly north side Royal Academy'). Turn left on to Stratton Street, and then right onto Piccadilly.

Green Park station opened as **Dover Street** in 1906 as part of the Great Northern, Piccadilly & Brompton Railway (GNP&BR), the route of which now forms much of today's Piccadilly line. The station originally included its own above-ground building, located close by at the junction with the street of the same name. It was designed by the great architect Leslie Green, whose distinctive ox-blood-red station designs came to define the aesthetic style of the Underground network, many fine examples of which still exist today.

Down Street tube station, used by Churchill's war cabinet in World War II.

When the station was redeveloped in 1933, the original building fell out of use, replaced instead by the sub-surface entrances and ticket hall seen today. It was also at this time that the station name was officially changed to Green Park. Nothing remains of the original building on Dover Street.

Head down Piccadilly, keeping to the right hand side of the road, and after a few minutes, turn right on to Down Street. On the left, a typical Leslie Green style building, now home to a newsagent, is the remains of **Down Street** tube station. Opened as part of the GNP&BR in 1907, it suffered from a lack of passengers from the outset, likely due to its location off the main road and close proximity to Green Park station behind, and Hyde Park Corner station up ahead. Closure finally came in 1932, but that wasn't to be the end of its life just yet.

After first being converted for use as offices, the station's short distance from Whitehall made it the perfect location for secret War Cabinet meetings after the outbreak of World War II. The station was duly converted to accommodate everything from a telephone exchange to sleeping quarters, and Winston Churchill himself is said to have often used the new facility. The secretive nature of the station's new use meant that the abandoned platforms were bricked-up and hidden from passing trains. The brickwork can still be seen today, and is covered in the Piccadilly line tube journey later in this book. The remains of the station below ground have seen no other use since the end of the war, and it's said that much of the wartime enhancements remain in situ. In addition to the newsagent, the disused building also includes a fire exit door from the track below; a common feature of most abandoned tube stations.

Retrace your steps back onto Piccadilly and continue in the same direction as before. When you reach the Intercontinental Hotel on your right, just past the Hard Rock Cafe, enter the Park Lane subway that passes under the busy road junction above. Continue in a straight line and exit at the other end. Turn right at the top of the steps and continue on, passing Apsley House and the grand entrance to Hyde Park on the right. The road here has now become Knightsbridge.

Cross over to the other side of the road, passing the Lanesborough Hotel on the left. A little further along on the left is the disused **Hyde Park Corner** station building, under wraps at the time of writing while being converted into the ultra-chic Wellesley Hotel. It was another distinctive red Leslie Green creation, opened with the rest of the GNP&BR in 1906.

When the station was refurbished in 1932, the extra space needed for the replacement of the original lifts with escalators meant that the station had to be rebuilt, and it was moved to its current location below ground. This put the

Brompton Road side entrance. The original frontage was demolished in the 1970s.

original station building out of use, but it survived for many years as a restaurant before closing in 2010, ready for its transformation as part of the new hotel, which should see it restored to its former glory. It's perhaps worth noting that the disused parts of the station are alleged to be haunted, something that probably isn't likely to be mentioned when guests arrive at the so-called 'six star' hotel being built on top of it.

Continue along Knightsbridge, and then bear left onto Brompton Road, just after the entrance to Knightsbridge tube station. Continue on, passing Harrods and various other luxury stores until you reach the Brompton Oratory (officially known as the Church of the Immaculate Heart of Mary) on the right hand side of the road. Just before it, turn right onto Cottage Place. Here, immediately on the right, you'll see another Leslie Green building, which is now all that remains of **Brompton Road** tube station. Another stop on the original GNP&BR route, the station was open from 1906–1934 and was another victim of low passenger numbers, with some trains not even stopping there at all as far back as 1908.

This remaining part of the station was used by staff only and there was no entrance hall. Instead passengers would have entered the station via a proper frontage on Brompton Road itself, but sadly this part of the complex was demolished in the early 1970s. In common with Down Street, the station was used in the war as a control room, and had its platforms hidden from passing trains (their location is covered in the Piccadilly line tube journey).

Return to Brompton Road and continue in the same direction as before. Head straight on to where the road now becomes Thurloe Place, ignoring where Brompton Road bears off to the left. Continue where the road bears left opposite the magnificent entrance to the Victoria & Albert Museum, until you reach the end at Cromwell Place. Here on the left, in a parade of shops at a busy junction and opposite the entrance to Old Brompton Road, is **South Kensington** station. Next to the entrance is a disused part of the station building, instantly recognisable as another example of Leslie Green architecture.

Although the station has been open since 1868, originally serving lines that would later become today's District and Circle lines, the complex was extended for GNP&BR use when the line began operation in 1906. But just like at Hyde Park Corner, the replacement of lifts with escalators in the 1970s led to vast redevelopment that rendered the original entrance useless. It's now used as a ventilation shaft, but remains in perfect condition from the outside. South Kensington also has disused platforms inside the station, and these are included in the tube journey from Gloucester Road to Arsenal later in the book.

Now head down Onslow Square and continue until you reach the end at the junction with Fulham Road (at this point Onslow Square is actually now called Sydney Place). Turn right on to Fulham Road and head straight for roughly 20 minutes, admiring the elegant side streets of Chelsea along the way.

Chelsea and Fulham station's disused platforms opposite Chelsea FC's Stamford Bridge.

A short while after Hortensia Street is a bridge that carries the road over train tracks, and the area on the left hand side of the road just before the bridge was the former site of **Chelsea and Fulham** railway station. Cross the bridge and turn left down the alley on the opposite side of the road to the Stamford Gate entrance to Chelsea Football Club's Stamford Bridge stadium. Turn left again just before the block of flats, and the overgrown remains of the station's platforms can easily be seen through the railings in the wall of the car park.

The station opened in 1863 as part of the Birmingham, Bristol & Thames Junction Railway, which connected the area with the London and Birmingham Railway (L&BR) and the Great Western Railway (GWR). The line was later changed to the more suitable name of the West London Line, but never managed to attract much use. The line closed in 1940, leaving Chelsea and Fulham station to rot away. Today, trains again pass through the station site as part of the new West London Line run by London Overground.

Head back onto Fulham Road and retrace your steps back over the bridge, this time turning onto Hortensia Road itself. When you reach the end, turn left briefly onto King's Road and then turn right. Here the road splits in two. Bear right onto Tadema Road, ignoring Ashburnham Road which bears off to the left. As you walk along, the spectacle of the mighty **Lots Road Power Station** starts to come into view. It can be seen in all its glory at the end of Tadema Road and on Lots Road itself.

Opened in 1905, it was built to help power the lines of the various different companies that owned underground railways at the time. One of the biggest power stations in the world when it opened, it originally had four chimneys, similar to the more famous Battersea Power Station further down the river. The facility was powering almost the entire London Underground network by the time each of the various companies merged to form one organisation, although it often worked in conjunction with Greenwich Power Station (which also still exists). The building was finally decommissioned in 2002 when its machinery reached the end of its lifespan, and its future currently hangs in the balance as hungry property developers try to get permission, and perhaps finance, for its conversion.

After exploring the power station site, retrace your steps back up Tadema Road. Now cross over King's Road onto Gunter Grove, and then turn left on to Fulham Road. Enter the grounds of Brompton Cemetery via the gates on the right hand side of the road. One of the most peaceful places in London, it's worth exploring, with many famous graves including Samuel Cunard and Emmeline Pankhurst. Walk through the cemetery and out via the other end onto Old Brompton Road (if the cemetery is closed, an alternative route is to cross over Fulham Road at the end of Gunter Grove and head on to Finborough Road. Turn left on to Old Brompton Road at the end, where you'll reach the other cemetery entrance).

The former Lots Road power station near Chelsea Harbour.

Turn left out of the cemetery, and shortly after on the left hand side of the road you'll find **West Brompton** station. Opened in 1866 as another stop on the doomed West London Line, the station is actually two in one, and always has been, with rail services on one side, and tube services on the other (the Underground side of the station was opened in 1869 by the Metropolitan District Railway). The railway station side looked very different in its original form, and even had its own goods yard area. It remained derelict for years after closure in 1940, until it was redeveloped for re-introduction into service in 1999. The current station is passed through as part of one of the train journeys listed later. Almost nothing now remains of the original station site.

West Brompton marks the end of the walk. London Overground runs frequent trains to Clapham Junction, Willesden Junction and Stratford, with numerous interchanges along the way. The Underground side of the station is on the Wimbledon branch of the District line.

WALK 5

Rags to Riches: north-east London to the City

This walk follows a route through many areas that just a few decades ago were some of London's most run down, tortured by a long history of debauchery and destruction that goes back further than the days of Jack the Ripper. Step forward to today and the same streets are now buzzing with the city's trendiest spots, including Hoxton, Shoreditch and Brick Lane. The journey then heads towards the City of London, where an ever-growing collection of skyscrapers are steadily covering over the remains of a long gone rail network.

START: Angel (Northern line)

FINISH: Liverpool Street (Circle, Hammersmith & City, Metropolitan and Central lines, National Rail)

TIME: 1 hour, 15 minutes

Exit **Angel** tube station by turning left on to Upper Street, then left again on to City Road (ignoring where the road also bears off to the right on to Goswell Road). Just ahead, on the corner of Torrens Street, you'll find the original and now disused Angel station building. It was opened in 1901 by the City and South London Railway (C&SLR), which would later merge with the Charing Cross, Euston & Hampstead Railway (CCE&HR) to form what is now the Northern line.

The station was extensively rebuilt in 1992, with the entrance hall of today replacing the one seen here. The wooden hoardings and ugly corrugated metal sheets that hide the original building's frontage were added after closure, although it is unclear why, and it's now used for access by maintenance workers. Traces of the original walls can however still be seen along Torrens Street itself.

The remains of City Road station, between Angel and Old Street.

Continue along City Road, and after a few minutes, on the right side of the road you'll find the corner of Central Street and the depleted remains of **City Road** tube station. Another C&SLR station opened in 1901, it was doomed from the start, with very little passenger use. When extensive work was deemed necessary in the 1920s to widen the tunnels of stations on the line between Moorgate and Euston, its low usage meant it closed permanently in 1922.

The odd looking building you see today is the result of partial demolition in the 1960s that saw most of the original structure removed, with what remained being reconstructed into a ventilation shaft from the tunnels below. It's also at this point when the tall brickwork vent stack was added on top. Look at the building from a few metres back however, and it's not hard to imagine how it would have looked when it was open – the sad shell of what remains now leaving almost no trace of what it once was. Further parts of the building can also be seen from Moreland Street. The platforms below are clearly visible from passing trains, and these are included in the Stockwell to Golders Green/Kentish Town tube journey later in the book.

Keep walking along City Road until you get to the busy roundabout where it meets the junction with Old Street. Making sure you are on the left side of the road, turn left at the roundabout towards Old Street itself, pausing on the corner as you do so. Old Street tube and rail station is located under the roundabout itself, but this replaced an original building that stood above ground on this corner, roughly in the space just beyond the steps that lead down to the current station.

Like Angel and City Road, it was opened in 1901 by the C&SLR, with train services added in 1904 by the Great Northern & City Railway. The street-level station was demolished in the 1960s and replaced by the one used today.

Head down Old Street, bearing left after a minute or so, ignoring where the road veers off to the right as Great Eastern Street. Just before you reach the end of Old Street you'll find a rail bridge, under which can be seen the bricked up former entrances to **Shoreditch** main line station. The station building is further ahead on the corner, now home to the appropriately-named Old Shoreditch Station pub.

The station opened in 1865 as part of the North London Railway (NLR), which itself originated as the East & West

Side entrance to the old Shoreditch railway station.

India Docks & Birmingham Junction Railway. The station was on a line that terminated at Broad Street station on a section of the two-mile long Kingsland Viaduct. Closure of Shoreditch main line station came in 1940 after it was damaged beyond repair in the Blitz, but the tracks above reopened to passing trains in 2010 as part of the new and improved East London line. Traces of the old platforms can still be seen trackside, and the site is included in the later train journey from Highbury & Islington to Whitechapel.

Now turn right on to Shoreditch High Street, continue for a few minutes and then turn right again, this time on to Holywell Lane. After walking under the rail bridge, look up on the left side of the road and you'll see two old tube train carriages marooned up high. Turn left at the end on to Great Eastern Street and you can now see them from the front. Used as trendy office space, the train carriages sit on an abandoned section of the Kingsland Viaduct, and the remains of where the tracks used to bridge the road can easily be seen in the brick work on both sides of the street. Built in the 1860s by the North London Railway, the viaduct closed over a century later in the 1980s, although parts of it were brought back into service when the East London line was re-launched in 2010. Continue along Great Eastern Street and stop when you reach the traffic lights. The partially re-developed area directly ahead, on Shoreditch High Street, between the corners of Commercial Road and Bethnal Green Road, is the former site of two different train stations and a vast goods yard, part of which is now home to London Overground's Shoreditch High Street station. The first station here was opened in 1840 under the name **Shoreditch** by the East Counties Railway (ECR). It was renamed Bishopsgate in 1847, and by 1862 the station was now operated by the Great Eastern Railway (GER). The opening of nearby Liverpool Street station in 1874 meant that most passenger services at Bishopsgate were withdrawn, and the facility was converted in to **Bishopsgate Goods Yard** in 1881.

Some GER services did still stop at the station however, and these were operated via a new set of platforms built below the goods yard. This new station was named **Bishopsgate (Low Level)**; although the suffix was dropped once the yard above had become established. Most of the entire complex was destroyed by fire in 1964 and remained derelict for decades after. Large-scale demolition came in 2004, although elements of the site now being Grade II listed have ensured that it is destined to be preserved.

Converted tube trains on the Kingsland Viaduct in Shoreditch.

Disused platforms of Bishopsgate low level station. The huge goods yard was on top.

Head left on to Shoreditch High Street, then turn right on to Bethnal Green Road, passing the massive concrete walls of Shoreditch High Street station that now covers huge parts of the Bishopsgate site. Stop at the entrance to Braithwaite Street on the right side of the road. From here, traces of the goods yard walls can be seen continuing along Bethnal Green Road. Head down Braithwaite Street itself, passing the entrance to the current station on your right.

After passing under the new tracks above, the road then passes under a second rail bridge. The brick arches on either side form part of the old goods yard and a stretch of the Braithwaite Viaduct; the street being named after its engineer John Braithwaite. As you pass under the bridge itself, gaps in the fencing on either side allow you to look directly into the disused goods yard site, with various decaying rooms and archways clearly visible. Parts of the Bishopsgate site can be seen from passing London Overground trains, and these are included in the rail journey from Highbury & Islington to Whitechapel later in the book.

When you emerge from the other side of the bridge, turn left on to Quaker Street. Just after the row of shops on the left, you'll find a locked gate with steps leading down to train tracks. This marks the former entrance to the Bishopsgate Low Level station, fragments of the platforms of which still exist. Although not included in any of the train journeys in this book, the old platforms can easily be seen on the three minute ride from Liverpool Street to Bethnal Green when travelling on a National Express East Anglia train.

Follow Quaker Street until the end, then turn left on to Brick Lane, one of the most vibrant areas in London; where the local Bangladeshi community rubs shoulders with weekend tourists and a fashion scene that's either super cool or super pretentious – the jury is still out.

After the row of shops along the right side of the road you'll

Shoreditch Underground station, closed in 2006 and now covered with graffiti.

find an alleyway named Pedley Street, which may or may not be signposted, but is easily recognisable by its street art-covered walls and the ever-present aroma of stale urine. It becomes wider at the end, and on the left you can find the closed **Shoreditch** tube station building, covered in graffiti.

It was opened in 1869 by the East London Railway, which was later incorporated into the Underground network as the East London Line, running southwards from here to stations at New Cross and beyond. The entire line was closed in 2006 for major refurbishment that saw it switch to become part of the new London Overground service. Shoreditch was the only station on the route that didn't re-open, replaced instead by the new Shoreditch High Street station seen earlier.

Looking more like a quaint church hall than a railway station, the tattered bunting hung outside on the final day of service could still recently be seen; the only clue left as to what the building once was. It stood abandoned for five years after closure, but was auctioned off in 2011 and at the time of writing was being used sporadically as a makeshift nightclub that had some creative new uses for the ticket hall signage still inside. The platforms were situated in a cutting below, but these have now disappeared. The various derelict wall fragments seen on the left just after the old tube station, under and on either side of the rail tracks, are all that now remains of **Spitalfields Goods Yard**, which operated as an extension of the facilities at Bishopsgate.

Retrace your steps back down Pedley Street, turn left back on to Brick Lane and follow it until it becomes Osborn Street, at which point turn left instead on to Old Montague Street. Next, turn right on to Davenant Street, and then right again at the end, on to Whitechapel Road. The car showroom on the other side of the road sits on the former site of **St Mary's** Underground station, opened in 1884. It was on a line that was operated as a joint venture between the Metropolitan Railway (MR) and the Metropolitan District Railway (MDR), much of which is now the District line. It was actually built by the East London Railway however, and it was their trains that used it first.

Its name changed to St Mary's (Whitechapel Road) in 1923, but was closed in 1938 after Aldgate East tube station was moved to a new location that made St Mary's redundant. It was brought back into use soon after as an air raid shelter but, perhaps ironically, it was destroyed by a bomb itself in 1940 and was demolished soon after. All that now remains is an emergency exit door that can be seen at the far right of the car showroom's forecourt, close to where it meets the wall of the East London Mosque next door. Some traces of the platforms can still be seen below ground – see tube journey later, from Tottenham Court Road to Whitechapel.

Head down Whitechapel Road, making sure you are on the right side of the road. A minute or so after passing **Aldgate East** station, stop when you reach the corner of Goulston Street. The derelict area behind the fence on the corner marks the location of the original Aldgate East station building, originally opened in 1884 as part of the same line as St Mary's. The station was demolished and rebuilt in 1914, before then being demolished a second time when it was resited in 1938 to the current station used today. Although the building is long gone, derelict traces of its sub-surface layout can still be seen from the street. Parts are also included in the same Underground journey as St Mary's.

Continue along Whitechapel Road, then bear right just after the old station site, on to St Botolph Street. Bear right again where the road becomes Houndsditch. Follow all the way to the end, including where Houndsditch becomes a much narrower street. Turn right on to Bishopsgate, then left soon after on to Liverpool Street. Walk along, keeping the train station on your right, and continue straight until you reach the corner of Eldon Street. The office building with the rounded frontage sits on what was roughly the location of **Broad Street** station, once one of London's biggest termini, with nine platforms. It was opened in 1865 by the North London Railway, closed in 1986, and demolished soon after to make way for the huge Broadgate Complex. Just beyond the office building is a sculpture made of iron girders, commemorating the location's former history as a main line railway station.

Retrace your steps back up Liverpool Street and enter Liverpool Street station itself for the end of the walk. It was opened in 1875 under the name Bishopsgate, before being given its present name in 1909, and has some disused elements of its own. Enter the tube station and head for the Circle, Hammersmith & City and Metropolitan line platforms. Although almost now hidden from view, parts of a disused bay platform can still be seen at one end of the platforms.

WALK 6

A City at War: south London's deep-level shelters

This walk starts by exploring what remains of stations that spread from one of London's most important rail terminals, south across the river and beyond. After that the route turns its attention to four of London's deep-level shelters. These were additional tunnels built under eight existing tube stations in the early 1940s, originally used by the government. Five of them were later opened to the public as air-raid shelters that protected thousands of people from Hitler's bombs. The plan was to use them after the war for a fast new limited stop underground line beneath the existing Northern line, but this never happened. The shelters remained largely empty for years after the war, although one of them ended up playing a key role in shaping the multi-cultural London of today. The last few years have seen most of them converted into use as facilities for archives and data storage.

START: Victoria (Circle, District and Victoria lines, National Rail)

FINISH: Clapham South (Northern line)

TIME: 2 hours

Start at **Victoria**, a station that has served as one of the great London termini ever since it opened in 1860, with the Underground first serving it in 1868. Exit via the main entrance of the main line station and turn left on to Terminus Place. Turn left again at the end, on to Buckingham Palace Road. Continue on, keeping Victoria on your left. After roughly ten minutes, continue on over the junction with Ebury Bridge and Pimlico Road, at which point the street now becomes Ebury Bridge Road.

Abandoned station building at Grosvenor Road near Victoria.

Follow until you reach the end, then turn left on to Chelsea Bridge Road. Just before the bridge itself heads over the Thames, turn left on to Grosvenor Road. Immediately after walking under the rail bridge, the building on the left is the disused **Grosvenor Road** station, opened in 1867 by the London, Chatham and Dover Railway (LC&DR). Three years later, the London Brighton & South Coast Railway (LB&SCR) added its own services to the station, but by 1911 trains on both lines no longer stopped here, and the station was closed. Currently, trains still run through the station site, and it's included in the rail journey from Victoria to Lewisham that appears later in the book. The area next to the old station building is now used as a depot and sidings for Victoria station.

Cross over to the other side of the road for amazing views across the river of the iconic Battersea Power Station, a Grade II listed building that has occasionally been used for events since it was decommissioned in the 1980s. Head back towards Chelsea Bridge, pausing just after you walk back under the rail bridge.

The area on the other side of the river, to the right of the railway bridge and now occupied by a block of expensive apartments, is the former site of two stations. Despite being on the wrong side of the river from its namesake, a station called **Pimlico** came first, opened in 1858 by the West End of London & Crystal Palace Railway (WELCPR) (see Walk 9). It served as the temporary terminus of the line before services were extended by parent company the LB&SCR over the river on the bridge seen today, and into Victoria.

Pimlico was closed shortly after in 1860, and the site was then used as **Battersea Wharf** goods depot, whose later expansion included the demolition of what remained of Pimlico. The yard itself has also now completely disappeared.

Now turn left on to Chelsea Bridge and cross over London's mighty river, at the other end of which the road becomes Queenstown Road. Turn left when you reach the roundabout, passing the petrol station. Then head under the rail bridge and on to Prince of Wales Drive. The walls running along the left at this point are part of the power station complex. Bear left at the end on to Battersea Park Road, and under the bridge are the remains of **Battersea Park Road** station, with three sealed doorways easily visible on either side of the road. It was opened in 1867 by the LC&DR under the name Battersea Park (York Road). It was changed to its final name in 1877, but closed in 1916 after a decline in passenger numbers.

Head back towards the junction with Prince of Wales Drive,

Former site of Battersea Park Road station, close to the famous dog's home.

but this time continue on down Battersea Park Road. Just before the next rail bridge, on the right side of the road opposite the Masons Arms pub, the wooden door surrounded by a brick arch hides the dilapidated parts of **Battersea Park** station, still open today. Sealed doorways on either side of the bridge as you walk underneath also hint at parts of the station no longer used. The station entrance lies on the other side of the bridge, although platform 5 is now rarely used.

Pass under the second bridge and then turn left, back on to Queenstown Road. After a minute or so you'll find **Queenstown Road** station. Enter the ticket hall, noticing as you do so that the brick work above the entrance still shows its original 1877 name of Queen's Road. Head up to platform 2, and across the other side of the tracks can be seen the now disused platform 1, made almost entirely out of wood. At the end of platform 2 you'll also find an abandoned signal box.

Return to the street and continue along in the same direction you were heading before, and then bear left on to Silverthorne Road when you reach the Victoria pub. After a few minutes the road ascends a slight hill, at the top of which turn left on to Wandsworth Road. A minute or so after passing Wandsworth Road station, turn right on to Union Road and follow it all the way to the end, including where it continues after the junction with Larkhall Rise and Larkhall Lane.

At the end of the road turn left on to Clapham Road, and after roughly five minutes you'll arrive at **Stockwell** tube station on the Northern and Victoria lines. The station is on the site of the southern terminus of the first deep level electric tube railway in the world, whose northern terminus was **King William Street.** The station is also one of the eight with deep-level shelters, and one of the five used by the public during the war. If you turn left just after the station entrance, on to Binfield Road, then left again on to Studley Road, you will find the southern entrance to the shelter – a circular concrete and brick structure – hidden behind the lock-up garages at the corner of Levehurst Way. It was opened in 1942, and like the other shelters, the complex below includes two wide tunnels that typically sit below the station platforms. It included a range of facilities for the thousands of people who sat there for hours during terrifying bombing campaigns, and is now used for archive storage.

Retrace your steps back to the tube station, and on the left where the road splits into South Lambeth Road and Clapham Road, the small park in the middle is where you'll find the north entrance to the shelter. Similar in design to the other end, this one has been painted by local schoolchildren and now appears to be used by the storage company as an emergency exit.

Head back down Clapham Road in the same direction from where you came, passing Stockwell station again, but this time continue straight, past the junction with Union Road.

Deep level shelter entrance at Clapham North station.

After a few minutes on the right side of the road you'll find the northern entrance to the **Clapham North Deep Level Shelter**; a similar-looking round building to those at Stockwell, located on the corner of an un-signposted slip road that leads to a car park for the block of flats named Clapham Road Estate.

Continue on, before then turning left on to Bedford Road just before the entrance to Clapham North station itself. Although sadly now part of a locked courtyard, behind the black doors next to Charlie's Fish Bar hides the southern entrance to the shelter.

Turn right on to Lendal Terrace, then left and back on to the main road, which is now Clapham High Street. After approximately five minutes, on the corner of a narrow street on the left named Carpenters Place, you can find the northern entrance to the **Clapham Common Deep Level Shelter**. It is hidden behind billboards but is still easy to see, and it actually infringes on part of the busy pavement, with shoppers passing by blissfully unaware.

Keep walking along, and the southern entrance can be seen on the corner at the junction with Clapham Common South Side and Clapham Park Road (not signposted), again partially hidden by billboards. Clapham Common tube station itself is just ahead in the middle of the junction. It has one of the most unique station entrance buildings on the whole of the Underground network, and used to be the terminus of what later became the Northern line before it was extended further south to Morden.

Now head on to Clapham Common South Side and keep straight, with the common itself on your right. After a few minutes you'll cross the entrance to The Avenue, and on the corner, inside the common, you can see the northern entrance to the **Clapham South Deep Level Shelter**, another that is now used for archive storage. Continue on, passing the entrance to the tube station itself, where the road now changes to Balham Hill. Just after the row of shops on the right side of the road you'll arrive at the southern entrance to the shelter. It's located in a locked courtyard owned by the archive company, but can clearly be seen from the street.

The shelter at Clapham South helped build the foundations of today's society when in 1948 it provided temporary accommodation to over 400 immigrants from Jamaica. They had arrived via boat on the Empire Windrush; encouraged to make the long voyage by the offer of work and a better life in London. The new arrivals looked for employment at the nearest job centre to Clapham South, which at the time was in

The deep level shelter at Clapham South was a temporary home for the 'Windrush generation'.

Brixton. The so-called 'Windrush Generation' gradually began to settle in the area, the legacy of which is today's well-established British Afro-Caribbean community that now spreads across London and the entire country. Return to Clapham South tube station for the end of the walk. The building is one of many designed by architect Charles Holden, whose unique designs can still be seen across many stations on the Northern and Piccadilly line.

Clapham South is on the Northern line on the branch to Morden. It's five stops away from Kennington, where interchange is available onto both the Charing Cross and Bank branches. Alternatively, National Rail services can be connected with by travelling one stop to Balham.

The other deep-level shelters are included in other walks as follows: **Camden Town** (Walk 3), **Goodge Street** (Walk 2) and **Chancery Lane** (Walk 1) The one at **Belsize Park** station is covered in the More Things to See miscellaneous section.

WALK 7

The Dirty Brick Road: Southwark's viaducts and bridges

This walk follows large parts of what is perhaps the greatest railway viaduct in the world. It runs for a distance of more than four miles from London Bridge to Deptford Creek, with more than 800 arches built out of millions of bricks by the hands of over 400 men between 1834–1836. It's also a journey through the Borough of Southwark, covering one of the city's oldest districts, before then heading South-West to Lambeth.

START: Bermondsey (Jubilee line)

FINISH: Brixton (Victoria line and National Rail)

TIME: 2 hours, 30 minutes

Exit Bermondsey tube station on to Jamaica Road. Turn right on to Keetons Road, left on to Perryn Road, then right again, this time on to Drummond Road. Walk to the end, until you come to the junction with Southwark Park Road. Turn left on to Southwark Park Road and then immediately turn right on to Raymouth Road (the street wasn't signposted at the time of writing but is easily recognisable by the viaduct and its arches running along its length on the right side of the road).

At the end of the street, when you reach the corner of Rotherhithe New Road, the area under the bridge is the abandoned **Southwark Park** station, opened in 1902 by the London and Greenwich Railway with platforms on the viaduct itself. It closed in 1915, followed a few years later by the rest of the line. Bricked-up doorways can clearly be seen under the bridge on both sides of the road, along with several former windows along Corbett's Passage. Head under the bridge, and the remains of a more significant former entrance can be

Bricked up windows of Southwark Park station in Bermondsey.

seen on the left, on Jarrow Road. The location of the old plat-
forms is included in the train journey from London Bridge to
Deptford later in the book, along with much of the viaduct.
There was also another station close by named **Commercial
Docks** from 1856–1867, but this is long gone.

Continue along Rotherhithe New Road, pausing briefly to look
inside the entrance to Rotherhithe Business Estate on the
right side of the road, just before the next bridge. From here,
it's clear that the great viaduct now splits into two directions.
This was one of several extensions to the original viaduct
route, opened in 1839 by the London and Croydon Railway. It

connected with the original route at nearby Corbett's Junction, one of the earliest examples in the world of a major railway junction.

Head under the next bridge and continue straight. The third bridge, on the corner of Galleywall Road, is where the first **South Bermondsey** station was located. Opened in 1866, the original building was demolished and replaced in the 1920s by the station that still exists today, its entrance being located on the other side of the bridge. The track above is no longer in use, leaving the bridge marooned as a forgotten relic of a long lost line.

Turn on to Galleywall Road and head straight. When you reach the end, turn left on to Southwark Park Road, then right again on to Bombay Street, where various derelict arches under the viaduct can be seen along the right side of the road. Follow to the end and turn right on to Blue Anchor Lane (unsigned), where more derelict parts of the structure can be seen. Turn right and head under the bridge, on to St James's Road. The bridge appears to have its own sealed doorways, although little is known about what used to be behind them. Turn left on to Linsey Street, and the various bricked-up arches under the dank bridge ahead formed part of the abandoned **Spa Road** station. Retrace steps back to St James's Road and continue in the same direction as before. Just after the St James Tavern, a small street on the left named Priter Road acts as the entrance to Discovery Business Park. Enter the complex, and directly ahead you'll find the remains of the station entrance, complete with 'Booking Office' and 'SE&CR' still written on the wall. The tracks above are still used, and are included in the London Bridge to Deptford train journey.

The station was opened in 1836 by the London and Greenwich Railway, acting as a temporary terminus for the line along the viaduct from Deptford before the final stretch to London Bridge was completed later in the year. The remains of the original building lie further ahead, and the one seen today is

Former entrance of the second Spa Road station building.

actually a replacement built in 1867 by the South Eastern and Chatham Railway, hence the SE&CR lettering on the wall. The new station had its name changed to Spa Road & Bermondsey in 1877, and it lasted until 1915 when it was closed after losing many of its passengers to competition from trams. There is also a round plaque above the entrance that pays tribute to the history of the station.

Return to St James's Road and continue along, then turn left onto Dockley Road and under the next bridge. Bear right, and at the end turn right again, this time onto Rouel Road. Now turn right on to Spa Road itself, and the bridge ahead marks the location of the original station. Bricked-up doorways can clearly be made out, and there is now a huge black and white photo of how it used to look attached to the wall.

Head back to Rouel Road and continue along, bearing left up ahead on to Enid Street, keeping the viaduct on your right. Next; turn left at the end on to Abbey Street, finally leaving the viaduct behind. Continue on after where it crosses Tower Bridge Road and Bermondsey Street shortly after, at which point the name of the road changes to Long Lane (not sign-posted). It is a street that lives up to its name, but also one of the finest examples of what makes London such an inter-esting place. The type of street where the forgotten history of the past battles with modern buildings, and where the affluent live right next door to the not so fortunate.

Where the road ends, bear right on to Great Dover Street, then left on to Borough High Street, passing Borough tube station on the right. After a few minutes, turn right on to Borough Road. When you reach the bridge, the area under the viaduct on the right side, now home to Long Lane Cab Centre, is the former **Borough Road** station. It was opened in 1864 by the London, Chatham and Dover Railway (LC&DR) as part of an extension to their City Line.

Having previously terminated at Blackfriars Bridge (see Walk 1), the line now ran all the way to Herne Hill, with a number of new stations along the way. Closure came in 1907 as a result of competition from nearby tube stations along what is now London Underground's Northern Line. The entrance to the cab company's office is also where the station's entrance would have been, and various dilapidated parts of the building can be seen down a dingy alley just after the former station site.

Now walk under the bridge and turn left on to Southwark Bridge Road. Bear left towards the end, before then turning right on to Newington Causeway. Navigate the busy road junction ahead by first bearing right and crossing the road in front of Elephant & Castle tube station. Now head in to the

Partial remains of Borough Road railway station.

subway system and follow signs for Elephant and Castle Road. You should emerge from the subway with the Metropolitan Tabernacle Baptist church just ahead, and the other entrance to Elephant & Castle tube station across the road on the left. Cross over to the other side of the road and left on to Walworth Road. It's not signposted but is easily recognisable as being flanked by the sorry-looking Elephant and Castle Shopping Centre on one side, and the ultra-modern Strata building on the other.

Continue walking along for roughly ten minutes, noticing as you do so that the road is running parallel with a rail viaduct that can be seen by looking down any of the streets off to the right. Turn right when you reach John Ruskin Street, and the

The dirty but still intact Camberwell station building.

area to the right of the bridge ahead is the former location of **Walworth Road** station, another of the stops on the City Branch extension. Opened in 1863 as Camberwell Gate, the name was changed just two years later, but what was meant to be a temporary closure in 1916 during World War I ended up being permanent. Nothing now remains of the station building.

Return to Walworth Road and continue on, although now the name of the street has changed to Camberwell Road. After about ten minutes the road comes to a busy junction. Turn right here on to Camberwell New Road, then left onto Camberwell Station Road. The viaduct runs along the right, with almost every commercial unit under its arches now being home to a car repair shop. Further along, a dirty white building opposite the bus depot, again used as a mechanics, is the disused **Camberwell** station. Yet another stop on the LC&DR branch, it opened in 1862 and closed in 1916. The largely intact building includes various bricked-up windows and doors that are easy to spot.

Continue until you reach the end, at which point turn left on to

Denmark Road, then right soon after on to Carew Street, where the viaduct runs low and closer to the street. Turn left at the end, away from the viaduct and on to Lilford Road (not signposted), then right on to Flaxman Road. At the end, turn right on to Coldharbour Lane, and just after the second bridge you'll find **Loughborough Junction** station. Although still open, there are disused and derelict platforms that can easily be seen from the current platforms. These are the remains of the section of the station served by the City Branch on its opening under the different name Loughborough Road in 1864 (the former platforms, along with those at Borough Road, Walworth Road and Camberwell are all passed through during the train journey from West Hampstead Thameslink to Herne Hill that appears later).

Head further along Coldharbour Lane, crossing over Loughborough Road, and then turn right on to Barrington Road. The Medusa Brixton Rock nightclub to the right of the bridge ahead is built into all that now remains of **East Brixton** station, opened in 1866 as part of the London, Brighton & South Coast Railway's South London Line. A series of name changes saw it go from being called Loughborough Park on its opening, to Loughborough Park and Brixton in 1870, until being changed one more time to the name that lasted until closure in 1976 after suffering competition from Brixton tube station close by. Although most of the station was demolished a few years after closure, there are a few bricked-up arches left. Trains still pass through the site, and its location is included in the train journey between Victoria and Lewisham.

Walk under the bridge and turn left on to Brixton Station Road, and then left again at the end, on to Brixton Road. A little further you'll find Brixton tube and rail stations, which signal the end of the walk. However the rail station itself also has a disused platform that includes the third of three sculptures of commuters.

WALK 8

Time Line to Forgotten Line: Greenwich and Lewisham

This journey follows what remains of a lost branch line from one of London's most important places. Although much has now disappeared without a trace, several areas along the route have seen many old main line railway lines come back into use as part of the Docklands Light Railway (DLR), the London Overground network and various other suburban train company lines. It is one of the many examples of London's ability to reinvent itself, always updating, while also paying tribute to days gone by.

START: Cutty Sark for Maritime Greenwich (Docklands Light Railway)

FINISH: Nunhead (National Rail)

TIME: 1 hour, 15 minutes

Exit Cutty Sark for Maritime Greenwich DLR station, opened in 1999 when the Docklands Light Railway was extended under the River Thames to Lewisham. Turn left in to the shopping precinct, then right on to Greenwich Church Street. Bear right past St Alfege Church, and the building on the corner of Stockwell Street, now home to Cafe Rouge and the Ibis Hotel, is the former site of **Greenwich Park** station. This opened in 1888 as the terminus of the Greenwich Park Branch, which was operated by the London, Chatham and Dover Railway (LC&DR). The entire branch line was closed in 1917 in the latter stages of World War I, leaving this and a number of other stations to become abandoned. The station building at Greenwich Park has long since been demolished with no trace at all left to suggest it was ever a station. The platforms themselves would have been located roughly on what is now the hotel car park.

Continue to bear right along Greenwich Church Street, then head left just after Greenwich London College and on to Greenwich South Street. When you reach the end, turn left at the junction on to Blackheath Hill. On the right side of the road, opposite to Plumbridge Street, the brick wall with an arched black doorway at the end is now all that remains of the former **Blackheath Hill** station. Another stop on the former branch line, it opened in 1871 as its temporary terminus until the station at Greenwich Park was ready for use (although this wouldn't be for another 17 years).

Retrace your steps back to the junction and now continue straight on to Blackheath Road. Bear left at the junction with Greenwich High Road on to Deptford Bridge, pass under Deptford Bridge DLR station and head straight on. Next, turn left on to Brookmill Road, then right on to St John's Vale. Head up the hill, passing St Johns station on the left. It is a pretty little station that's well worth a look, including a footbridge to the platforms that provides a great view of trains running in and out of London. It's been open since 1873, but the original complex was demolished in the 1970s and replaced with what you see today. It also has the ominous distinction of being the closest station to the location of the Lewisham rail crash that killed 90 people in 1957 – still one of the worst post-war rail accidents in Britain.

Turn left at the top on to Lewisham Way. Just after where the road crosses a bridge over rail tracks below, the street changes to now being called Loampit Hill. The building on the left after the bridge is the old **Lewisham Road** station, now home to an antiques and bric-a-brac shop named Aladdin's Cave. It was another of the stations on the Greenwich Park Branch, which opened with the others in 1871, and closed in 1917.

The shop that now uses the building is full of treasures and a great place to explore. It also provides you with the rare opportunity to actually go inside an abandoned train station.

Lewisham Road station, now a quirky antiques store.

The owners have even paid tribute to its former use with photos on the wall of how it once looked. Peering over the bridge itself also gives you the chance to see various arched doorways at track side where the platforms once sat. Trains began running through the site again in 1929, veering right further ahead towards the Lewisham rail and DLR station in operation today. This is included in the train journey later on from Victoria to Lewisham.

Entrance steps to Brockley Lane. Most of the building was destroyed by fire.

Head back over the bridge to the corner of St Johns Vale, but now continue straight and along Lewisham Way. Next, turn left on to Breakspears Road, right on to Ashby Road, left again down Wickham Road and then right on to Geoffrey Road. Continue to the end before turning left on to Brockley Cross. The building on the left, next to the Brockley Cross street sign, is the old **Brockley Lane** Station Master's house.

The station building itself was destroyed by fire in 2004, but was located in the derelict area across the road, between the rail bridge and the Prestige barber shop. It opened a year after the station at Lewisham Road in 1872, as the final stop on the branch line before the terminus at Nunhead. It closed with the rest of the line in 1917, but was used right up until 1970 as a goods yard. A few traces of the station are still visible, including steps up to what would have been the entrance. As with Lewisham Road, trains still run through the site of the old platforms above, and these are included in the same train journey.

Brockley Road stationmaster's house. The derelict station itself lies across the road.

Original site of Nunhead station.

Turn back, and now turn left onto Endwell Road, bear right and then turn left on to Drakefell Road. After an ascent uphill, the road begins to slope down again, at which point great views of the ever-changing London skyline can be seen in the distance. Turn left on to Kitto Road, then right when the street now becomes Gibbon Road. Turn left at the end, and on the right, just after the rail bridge, you'll find the entrance to **Nunhead** station.

It was opened in 1871 by the LC&DR, serving both their Greenwich Park Branch and the Crystal Palace and South London Junction Railway (see Walk 9 for more on this line). Platforms for these lines were part of an original station building that was located on the opposite side of the road from the entrance of today, before it was closed in 1925, resited to the other side of the road and subsequently demolished. Go in to the current station, and you can see where the former platforms would have been by looking back towards the bridge over the road from the end of platform 2. This is included in the journey from Victoria to Lewisham later on.

Nunhead marks the end of the walk. The station is served by Southeastern, with frequent trains running back to Victoria and various other suburbs.

WALK 9

The Rise and Fall of a Victorian Folly: the ghosts of Crystal Palace

This journey takes a trip to south London to follow what remains of a line that connected the suburbs to one of the greatest attractions in Victorian London. The Great Exhibition of 1851 was a celebration of the latest innovations from around the world, and it was all housed inside the Crystal Palace, a huge glass and metal structure engineered by Joseph Paxton. Originally located in Hyde Park, the palace was dismantled after the fair ended, shipped to Sydenham Hill and rebuilt on an even grander scale than before. Two stations were built close by to cash in on the thousands of expected visitors, including an elegant terminus adjacent to the new palace site. Although a success at first, the public's interest had mostly dried up by the time the palace was destroyed by fire in 1936, and it was this same disaster that led to the demise of its grand station and the line it served.

START: Crystal Palace (National Rail)

FINISH: Honor Oak Park (National Rail)

TIME: 2 hours

Start at **Crystal Palace** station, one of the two competing buildings built for visitors to the palace. It was opened in 1854 by the West End of London & Crystal Palace Railway (WELCPR), itself operated by the London, Brighton & South Coast Railway (LB&SCR). Officially known as Crystal Palace (Low Level), to differentiate it from the competing station close by, the downfall of the palace inevitably led to a huge drop in passengers that resulted in some lines that previously stopped at the station now being diverted elsewhere.

Disused parts of Crystal Palace station – a bay platform and the original entrance building which is now used as offices.

Although the station is still open, it does currently have some disused parts, including bay platforms and grand concrete staircases, all of which can easily be seen from the current platforms. Most of the original building was taken out of use when it was replaced in the 1980s with the more low-key entrance hall used today, although it was restored in 2002 and is now used as office space.

Exit the station and head left down Crystal Palace Station Road. Next, turn right on to Anerley Hill, keeping the park where the palace once stood on your right. When you reach the top, turn right on to Crystal Palace Parade, then left on to Farquhar Road. Cross over to the right side of the road and look over the blue railings at the buildings below. This is the former site of the now demolished **Crystal Place (High Level)** station, opened in 1865 by the Crystal Palace and South London Junction Railway, owned by the London, Chatham and Dover Railway (LC&DR).

When you look down at the site from here, with no trace left of what it once was, it's hard to imagine that it used to be one of London's most luxurious and stylish stations. Its location, literally across the road from the palace, gave it the advantage over the Low Level station, and the building itself was built in a lavish style that befit its famous neighbour.

The line ran from here to Nunhead and proved popular at the height of the palace's success. But the following decades were not so kind, with a huge drop in numbers, reduced services, temporary closures and name changes (it was known as Crystal Palace High Level and Upper Norwood from 1898–1923). Permanent closure came in 1954 along with the rest of the line, and the station was demolished in the early 1960s.

The only visible part of the station complex that does still exist is the retaining wall, which can be seen from here, running along the right, with Crystal Palace Parade above.

You can also see the remains of concrete steps above the wall, just before the above road curves onto Farquhar Road. These were part of a side entrance to the station.

Continue on down Farquhar Road, and then turn right onto Bowley Close. This is where the entrance to the station building would have been, and the retaining wall can be seen more closely from here. Now head towards the wall and turn left, and just before it turns into a series of arches, you can see the bricked-up remains of an entrance to a subway that would have ran under the road. This was the more elegant station entrance that led directly to the palace grounds.

Retrace steps back to Farquhar Road and continue on in the same direction you were headed before. This time turn right on to Bowley Lane and walk to the end. When you reach the

Former side entrance to Crystal Palace High Level station, closed 1954.

Paxton tunnel, named after Crystal Palace engineer Joseph Paxton.

end, and therefore rejoin the retaining wall, turn left onto Spinney Gardens, a private but accessible road with houses running along the left. At the end, you'll find the now sealed southern portal of **Paxton Tunnel**, named after Crystal Palace engineer Joseph. It was built by the railway in 1865 as part of the route towards Sydenham, and is roughly 439 yards long.

Return to Farquhar Road and walk all the way back to the top where you started. This time turn left on to Crystal Palace Parade and walk along the left side. A bricked up gap in the wall can clearly be made out as you begin to walk, and behind this are the abandoned steps seen from Farquhar Road. Further along, where there is a break in the fencing with wall only, peering down at this point gives you chance to see the top of the bricked-up subway entrance seen earlier, along with another set of steps that would have led down from the road (a gap in the wall can again easily be seen).

Derelict subway that once led directly to Crystal Palace.

Cross over to the other side of the road, and from here you can look through the railings and see the derelict remains of the other end of the subway, and the steps that would have led to the palace. Sadly no longer accessible to the public, the subway itself is a Grade II listed structure, with an ornate vaulted roof.

Head along on this side of the road, keeping the park where the palace once stood on your right. As you walk along you can see the Crystal Palace Transmitter in all its glory; one of London's tallest structures and a landmark that's visible for miles. Bear right just after the tower, passing the entrance to Sydenham Hill, and on to Westwood Hill. Then turn left onto High Level Drive, and left again on to the unnamed street just after the block of flats named Pemberton House. Turn left again on to The Gradient, and behind the concrete football pitch you'll find the northern portal of the Paxton Tunnel.

This retaining wall is now all that remains of the Crystal Palace High Level station platform area.

Retrace steps back to Westwood Hill and continue in the same direction you were headed before. Turn left on to Longton Grove, then left again onto Longton Avenue, keeping the beautiful Sydenham Wells park on your right as the road bends and goes uphill. When you reach the top, turn left on to Wells Park Road, and the building a little further on the left numbered 151–158 is the old **Upper Sydenham** station building, still intact.

Another station on the line from Crystal Palace High Level, it was opened in 1884 and closed in 1954 with the others. It struggled to attract passengers even before the palace closed, as most people seemed to prefer to use nearby Sydenham and Sydenham Hill stations instead (both of which are still open today). It is still obvious looking at the building that it was once a station, with the forecourt area still clearly marked out, and steps down from the road at the far end.

The station building at Upper Sydenham, little used by passengers from the very start.

Walk down the steps, turn right and head down the path into Dulwich Woods (not signposted). As you walk along, the area that is now the station's garden would have been where steps led down to the platforms. Further along the path, directly below the station, you'll find the sealed southern portal of **Crescent Wood Tunnel**. Upper Sydenham's platforms were situated in the overgrown area directly in front of the tunnel mouth, and although demolished, a few small traces of them still remain visible on the right hand side of the tunnel entrance. There was also a footbridge in front of the tunnel connecting the two platforms, but of course this is also now long gone. The tunnel itself is 400 yards long.

Crescent Wood Tunnel northern portal, now used as a bat sanctuary.

Return to the station building and turn left, continuing up Wells Park Road. Turn right at the top, on to Sydenham Hill, ignoring the entrance to Crescent Wood on the left. After a few minutes, turn left at the other entrance to Crescent Wood, and along the railings on the right side of the road you'll find the entrance to Sydenham Wood Wildlife Trust nature reserve. Enter, and bear left at the information board. Follow the downward path until you reach a brick wall on the right. Here, you are standing on top of the northern portal of the Crescent Wood tunnel, and following the path even further brings you out at the tunnel mouth, which is now used by the trust as a habitat for bats.

Return to Sydenham Hill and continue along, bearing left when the road goes downhill at the junction with Kirkdale. The descent provides great views over central London, including the Heron Tower and the Shard, both competing to become the city's tallest building at time of writing. At the bottom of the hill, turn left on to London Road. The houses, grass mounds and lock-up garages of the Lapsewood Estate immediately on the left mark the former site of **Lordship Lane** station; another stop on the line between Crystal Palace and Nunhead, opened in 1865 (the road changes name to Lordship Lane a few metres ahead). Even before its closure in 1954 the station looked doomed, and had to shut its doors from 1944–1946 after suffering significant bomb damage in World War II. Nothing at all now remains of the station, although parts of the former track bed can be walked along inside Horniman Gardens on the other side of the road.

Next, turn right on to Wood Vale, opposite the old station site (sign post was missing at time of writing). Continue straight on, passing Camberwell Old Cemetery on the left after a few minutes. As you reach the end of the road, the blocks of flats that make up Lewisham Council's Woodvale Estate stand on the former location of **Honor Oak** station, which was the last stop on the line before the end of the branch at Nunhead. As the others, it opened in 1865 and closed in 1954, and nothing now remains.

Turn right on to Forest Hill Road, then left on to Honor Oak Park as you climb uphill. A few minutes after passing the grounds of Saint Augustine church and One Tree Hill on the left, the road begins to descend, and further along you'll find Honor Oak Park station, opened in 1886 by the LB&SCR.

This is the end of the walk. The station is served by London Overground, with regular trains to Highbury & Islington, Crystal Palace and West Croydon, and by Southern, who run frequent trains to London Bridge, Victoria, Clapham Junction and Caterham.

WALK 10

From Park to Palace: Northern Heights and beyond

Starting at Finsbury Park, this walk takes a journey across north London, ending in Wood Green at the historical Alexandra Palace. Much of the walk follows the route of a never-completed project partly developed in the 1930s for some main line branches to become part of the Underground's Northern Line. The onslaught of World War II, rising costs and declining passenger numbers meant that the works were never finished, and the demise of the stations along the proposed route followed a few years later. It was also to be a fate shared by a number of stations originally built to serve 'Ally Pally' in the decades after its glory had faded.

START: Finsbury Park (Piccadilly & Victoria lines, National Rail)

FINISH: Alexandra Palace (National Rail)

TIME: 2 hours

Leave Finsbury Park station via the main exit on Station Place. Turn left, and cross over to the other side of Stroud Green Road. Here you'll find the entrance to Finsbury Park itself, clearly signposted and easily recognised as being next to a modern-looking bike shed. Enter the park and bear left on the path, keeping the tennis courts and skate park on your right.

Exit the park when you reach a set of gates on the left where a sign marks the two mile distance to Highgate. Cross the rail bridge, and then turn right onto the path. This is the official start of the Parkland Walk, a beautiful stretch of well-kept public footpath that takes you along the former route of the Edgware, Highgate and London Line, owned by the Great Northern Railway (GNR); a company that was later absorbed

Stroud Green station building, still intact.

into the London and North Eastern Railway (LNER). The route takes you along the actual track bed itself, although the rails have long since been removed.

After bridging over Upper Tollington Park road below, the walk reaches a second bridge a short while later, and this marks the area where the platforms of **Stroud Green** station once sat. Leave the walk here briefly by taking the path down the bank on the right, just before the bridge itself. When you reach Lancaster Road at the bottom, turn left, and the building facing you, just to the right of the bridge itself, is the actual former station building, still intact and now used as a mental health centre. The station operated from 1881 until the entire line closed for passenger services in 1954. The branch was still used by freight trains until the late 1960s, before finally closing for good.

Retrace your steps back to the Parkland Walk and continue onto the bridge itself. Some faint elements of the platform area can still been, although there is no trace at all left of how these connected to the building below. Continue on, next passing the bridge over Mount Pleasant Villas, where various trackside elements can still clearly be seen. Up ahead, the path passes under two bridges and an adventure playground on the left. Just before you reach the next footbridge over the path, look at the graffiti-covered arches within the wall on the right hand side. Hiding inside one of the alcoves is a sculpture of a life-sized figure, literally coming out of the wall. It's the work of artist Marilyn Collins, and is said to have been inspired by the urban legend of a strange spriggan that haunted the area.

Just beyond the footbridge are the remains of what was once **Crouch End** station, opened in 1867 and closed in 1954. The remains of the platforms on either side can clearly be seen as you walk along the track. At the end of the platforms, the brick turrets on the road bridge above are all that remains of where the station building once sat, and steps up to the road from the right hand platform reveal how they would have been accessed from street level. Continue along under the bridge itself, later passing over two more bridges, including one where the road below is so narrow that cars have to pass under one at a time.

After a further stretch along which various old trackside elements can be seen under the overgrowth, the path ahead reaches the imposing portals of two tunnels. These are the now-abandoned **Highgate Tunnels,** which lead directly to the former Highgate station further beyond. Although locked, you can peer through the gates and see daylight at the other end. This marks the end of the Parkland Walk route for the time being.

For now, take the path bearing left just before the tunnels, which brings you out onto Holmesdale Road. Head right, then

Former platforms of Crouch End station on the Parkland Walk.

Spriggan sculpture hidden in the arches near Crouch End station.

Abandoned Highgate tunnels, leading to Highgate station.

Remains of Highgate high-level station, located above the Northern line tube station.

left up the hill, before turning right onto Archway Road. Cross Shepherd's Hill and walk down the sloped road that marks the entrance to Highgate tube station car park (ignore the sign telling you to continue along Archway Road for the next part of the Parkland Walk). Although too high to see over, the wall along the right hand side of the road disguises the other portals of the Highgate Tunnels seen earlier.

Enter Highgate tube station itself via the steps. Walk through the ticket hall and out of the station at the other end via Exit 2 (signposted for Priory Gardens). Take the steep footpath immediately on the left and stop after a few metres. Turn to your left and you'll see the overgrown and abandoned remains of **Highgate High Level**, directly above the tube station. The view is somewhat obscured by the station cottage and gardens, now a private residence, but the moss-covered platform canopy and platforms themselves can clearly be seen. The station was open to passengers from 1867–1954 and was built in a cutting, still evident today.

Tunnel portals at either end of the abandoned platforms can also easily be seen. One set belongs to the tunnel seen earlier that leads back to Crouch End, while the other tunnels mark where the line continued on towards Edgware and High Barnet.

Continue upwards on the footpath until it brings you out onto Wood Lane. Head left, then turn right onto Muswell Hill Road. Here the route descends downhill, with Highgate Wood running along the left hand side of the road. As you walk along, look down any of the roads leading off to the right for breathtaking views over London.

When you reach Cranley Gardens, the area on the left hand side of the main road marks the former site of **Cranley Gardens** station, now the location of flats and a school, centred around a path called Woodside Gardens. Originally opened as a small goods yard in 1897, it was expanded for passenger use from 1902 until its closure in 1954, and was the first stop on a short branch line that left the route towards Edgware and instead headed for Alexandra Palace. There are now no visible traces left of the long since demolished station.

Take the path that runs alongside the former station site and follow it under the road bridge, rejoining the Parkland Walk. After a short while, the path narrows onto a viaduct that provides sweeping views back towards central London all the way to Canary Wharf in the Docklands. The official route of the Parkland Walks ends a few minutes later, when you reach a subway that leads under Muswell Hill above. Take the subway and follow the path towards the right. The area on the left behind the railings, now home to Muswell Hill Primary School, is the site of the now demolished **Muswell Hill** station. It ran from 1873–1954 as part of the branch line to Alexandra Palace. Turn right onto Muswell Hill itself and head uphill for a few minutes before turning right again, this time onto Dukes Avenue.

Alexandra Palace station in front of the famous palace itself.

As you descend the hill, the imposing sight of Alexandra Palace itself begins to come into view, including the still-in-use TV mast, the original of which helped shape the history of television when the BBC made some of their first-ever public broadcasts from the palace in 1936.

Mid-way down Duke's Avenue as you head towards the palace, stop at the junction with Grove Avenue. On the right hand side of the road is an entrance to Alexandra Park, and from here you can clearly see a bridge crossing over the foot-path. No longer in use, the bridge is one of the few remains of how the train line reached the palace itself.

Continue along the street until you reach the end, and then turn right onto The Avenue. Just ahead, dwarfed by the palace itself is the old **Alexandra Palace** station building, still intact and now used as a community centre. One of three stations built to cash in on the expected success of the palace when it opened it 1873, this station had the commercial advantage of being the only one that brought passengers all the way to the palace itself. It was forced to close for a period of two years when the palace famously burned down just days after it opened, but would eventually be in service for over seventy years before finally closing with the rest of the line in 1954. Nothing remains of the platform area or track bed.

Head down The Avenue away from the station and palace, and then turn right onto Vallance Road. After that turn right onto Talbot Road, and right again onto Alexandra Park Road. Now bear left onto Palace Gates Road, heading over the bridge at the end, keeping the entrance to Bedford Road on your right. Make sure you walk along the left hand side of the road along the bridge, and as you do so, peer over the side for a view of the tracks down below. The sidings and train sheds are now home to Bounds Green depot, but part of the site was also the location of **Palace Gates** station. When you reach the end of the bridge, bear left onto Bridge Road, and the yard on the left (now occupied by a builder's merchant) is where the majority of the station once stood.

Originally opened in 1873 under its full name Palace Gates (Wood Green), the station was owned by the Great Eastern Railway (GER) and formed the terminus of its branch line from Seven Sisters. Another of the three stations built to serve Alexandra Palace, it proved to be unsuccessful, and saw its numbers dwindle even further with the opening of nearby Bounds Green and Wood Green tube stations, before eventually closing in 1964. Virtually nothing remains of the site, although some bricked-up structures near the entrance to the merchants may have been part of the original station complex.

Continue along Bridge Road, including where it bears right and becomes Dorset Road. Turn right at the end and head straight. At the end of the short street is the current Alexandra Palace station, located on Buckingham Road. Built in a similar

Continue Buckingham Road + Station Road to Wood Green tube station + change at Fins. Park.

A remaining structure on the site of the demolished Palace Gates station. Its original use is unknown but it is in a style that was common in the first world war period. It may have been a coal office.

style as the old station next to the palace, it was the third station built to serve the venue, but the only one still in operation today. Since opening in 1859, the station at various different times has been named both Wood Green and Wood Green (Alexandra Park), before finally settling with its current name in 1982. Your arrival at the station signals the end of the walk. Frequent trains run from here to Kings Cross and various other destinations.

WALK 11

Back From the Brink of Oblivion: the London Docklands

This walk takes you through the heart of the famous London Docklands, an area that is once again thriving after massive redevelopment in the last 20 years. But the echoes of its glorious past as one of the world's most important docks can still be heard in its street names and forgotten buildings. The route follows an abandoned railway line that ran through much of the area. Vast sections of the line have since been brought back to life by the Docklands Light Railway.

START: Canning Town (Jubilee line, Docklands Light Railway)

FINISH: King George V (Docklands Light Railway)

TIME: 2 hours

Start at **Canning Town,** a station with a long and colourful history. It was built as part of the East Counties and Thames Junction Railway (EC&TJR); a line that ran from Stratford to North Woolwich, with various small branch lines along the way. It later became part of what is now the North London Line, before being taken out of service completely in 2006.

Canning Town opened in 1846 under the name Barking Road and was located a short walk from today's station, roughly where Barking Road joins Newham Way. The name was changed to its present form in 1873, when the building was resited to a new location close to the end of Stephenson Street. Nothing remains of the first two station buildings, and the one seen today was built in 1995 when the station reopened to be serviced by the Jubilee line and the Docklands Light Railway (DLR). The platforms that served North London Line trains until 2006 were visible for a while after closure, but these went as the station was redeveloped further.

Former location of Tidal Basin station.

Exit via the bus station, following signs for the 'ExCeL Walking Route' (ExCeL being an exhibition venue close by). Head out on to Silvertown Way in the direction away from the station. After a few minutes, the road veers upwards on to the Silvertown Viaduct flyover. Keep straight, walking along the flyover itself on the right side of the road (despite it being a busy road, pedestrians are permitted to walk along the pavement on both sides of the flyover).

Towards the far end, just after where the road crosses over DLR tracks below, you'll see a bus stop on the right (serving bus number 474 from Canning Town to Manor Park). Just before this, a staircase leads off the flyover and down to another road below. Descend the stairs, turn left and head under the flyover. Immediately after, a footbridge over the rail tracks marks the location of the former **Tidal Basin** station. It was opened in 1857 as another stop on the EC&TJR route, but closed permanently in 1943 after suffering substantial damage during the Blitz. There are no remains left, although a strip of undergrowth just to the right of the bridge hints at where one set of platforms was sited.

Cross over to the other side of the footbridge, which brings you out on to Victoria Dock Road. Head straight, keeping the DLR tracks on your right as you walk along, passing Royal Victoria DLR station after a few minutes. Stop when you get to the corner of Freemasons Road, and on the right you'll find Custom House for ExCeL DLR station. This is also however the location of **Custom House** railway station, opened on the EC&TJR line in 1855 and closed with the others in 2006.

Although Crossrail will see the site radically redeveloped, there were plenty of the station's remains still visible at time of writing, including a boarded up entrance just beyond the current DLR station, complete with an abandoned ticket machine that read 'machine not working' in crude marker pen. The former track bed and platforms could also be seen by entering the DLR station, heading up the stairs and looking left through the windows on either side as you cross the bridge towards the current platforms.

Continue along Victoria Dock Road, where more traces can be seen of where the North Woolwich branch tracks used to run before being removed after closure. After a few minutes you'll reach Prince Regent DLR station on the right. Enter and head up the flight of steep stairs (or take the lift). When you reach the top, look out of the windows of the footbridge that leads to the platforms. On the right you can see the old track bed back towards Custom House. But through the left windows, you can clearly see where the track bed begins to descend into a cutting with walls on both sides. This is where trains used to disappear into the **Connaught Tunnel**. An impressive feat of engineering when it was built in 1878, the tunnel allowed trains to run across both the Albert and Victoria Docks without the need for bridges. By 1969 passenger trains only ran through the tunnel on one of the two sets of tracks, although the other set was used by freight trains until the early nineties. The tunnel was abandoned in 2006 with the rest of the line, but will be brought back into use as part of Crossrail.

Disused platforms at Custom House station, ready for redevelopment by the Crossrail project.

Return to the street and continue in the same direction you were headed before. Bear right when the pavement veers away from the road and up a verge. From the traffic lights at the top you'll see a Premier Inn hotel up ahead. The overgrown wasteland between the other side of the road and the hotel is the location of the former **Connaught Road** station, another lost stop on the EC&TJR.

In addition to the route ahead to North Woolwich, the line also split off in two other directions close by, with one branch towards **Beckton** and another to **Gallions**, of which Connaught Road was the first stop. Low passenger numbers led to its closure in 1940 and virtually nothing now remains except for a few fragments of concrete hidden in the undergrowth. There are also no remains left of any other station on the Gallions and Beckton branches. The line to Beckton included a goods yard at Beckon Gas Works, a huge former complex that has since been demolished, but which achieved fame after closure as an 'extra' in the film *Full Metal Jacket*.

Over the road from the old station site and to the right, you'll see the metal walls of a short bridge where the road curves. Peer over and you can see directly down into an open section of the Connaught Tunnel, including derelict tracks and concrete arches. It's a location that's been used several times on screen, including a chase scene in Guy Ritchie's 2008 gangster film *RocknRolla*.

Now head towards the Premier Inn, walk through its car park, under the elevated DLR tracks above and turn right on to Festoon Way (keeping the Ramada hotel on your right). As you continue towards the water, the flyover road to the left is the Connaught Bridge, beyond which can be seen aircraft on the tarmac of London City Airport, opened in 1987 on the redeveloped Royal Albert Docks. A series of brickwork columns under the flyover are ventilation shafts from the Connaught Tunnel below, which runs under the water just ahead.

Connaught Tunnel, used in the film 'Rocknrolla'.

The decaying remains of Silvertown railway station.

Cross the short footbridge over the water, pausing as you do so to look right for sweeping views over the old Royal Victoria Docks and on towards Canary Wharf. The huge abandoned building to the left is the old Spiller's Millennium Mills, perhaps one of the biggest derelict structures in London. It operated as the city's largest mill from the 1930s until 1992; closed down when the company followed many others to Tilbury Docks as the Docklands fell in to decline. Better views of this magnificent building can be seen from the platforms of Pontoon Dock DLR station.

When you reach the other side, bear left, under the road bridge and along the footbath back up to street level. Turn left at the roundabout on to Connaught Road and bear right, keeping the airport on your left. The concrete walls along the right side of the road conceal where the Connaught Tunnel ends and therefore where trains would have re-emerged from the darkness. As the road now bears left, the sight of the imposing Tate & Lyle refinery comes into view, but in the fore-ground you'll see a footbridge, and beyond it the sad remains of **Silvertown** station.

Another stop on the original EC&TJR and later North London Line, it opened in 1863 and closed in 2006. It was in a sorry state at time of writing, with derelict platforms and overgrown tracks that made it look as though it had been closed for decades. It's a scene perhaps made worse by the fact that the surrounding streets of Silvertown also look the same; a forgotten ghost town marooned between a busy airport and a factory that once employed hundreds from the estate. The station site is set to be cleaned up for Crossrail, but plans for a new station here appear to have been overlooked.

Silvertown was also the location of a huge disaster in 1917 when a factory close by exploded while making ammunitions for World War I. The blast killed 73 people and still ranks as one of Britain's worst industrial accidents. A memorial stands hidden on the pavement under the elevated DLR tracks between Silvertown West and Pontoon Dock stations. The efforts of policeman Edward George Brown Greenoft in helping victims of the explosion at the cost of his own life are honoured by a plaque in the emotional Memorial to Heroic Self Sacrifice in Postman's Park located in the City. Also remembered at the park are several men who lost their lives on the railways of the Victorian era.

Cross over the footbridge for a better look at the station site on one side and the route into the Connaught Tunnel on the other. When you come out of the other side of the bridge, turn left on to Factory Road. Look out for train tracks embedded in to the road here, plus the scant remains of what used to be a level crossing. These are the only traces left of the Silvertown Tramlink, a basic tram line that ran from factory to factory after the EC&TJR route was redirected through the tunnel. Now head along Factory Road, keeping the refinery on your right and the old station site on your left. The derelict remains of the tracks can be seen along the way, as well as a lonesome looking footbridge over them further along. When you reach the end of the road, turn right on to Store Road, passing the Thames Water plant on the left.

Next, turn left on to Pier Road, past the Woolwich Ferry car terminal on the right, and then bear right until you reach a sharp bend to the left. On the corner you'll find the well preserved original **North Woolwich** station building. It was opened in 1847 as the terminus of the EC&TJR line, and survived in use until 1979. At this point, by now part of the North London Line, it was replaced by an ugly looking wooden entrance that matches those at Custom House and Silvertown. The boarded up remains of this could also still be seen at time of writing, located just before you reach the 1847 building.

The original station was given a new lease of life as the North Woolwich Old Station Railway Museum, although this also sadly closed in 2008. The platforms still remain in situ, but these are no longer visible to the public. There was also a small station on the side of the Thames known as **North Woolwich Pier**, which used to allow passengers to change from ferry services on to trains at the main station. The burned out and vandalised remains of this can be seen by walking down the concrete steps opposite the North Woolwich station site.

Bear left round the station and continue along Pier Road. Keep straight over where it crosses Albert Road, and soon after you'll arrive at **King George V** DLR station and the end of the walk. The station opened in 2005 as part of an extension to Woolwich Arsenal that was completed in 2009.

It's on the Woolwich Arsenal branch of the DLR, with frequent trains back to both Bank and Tower Gateway in central London, and interchange with the Jubilee line along the way at Canning Town.

Original North Woolwich station buiding, later a railway museum (now closed).

Closed 1970s North Woolwich station entrance.

WALK 12

The Real Eastenders: walking the Tower Hamlets

This walk takes you on a trip through much of what makes up the true East End of London, covering many areas yet to be included in the rampant redevelopment schemes that have transformed vast parts of the nearby Docklands. There have been some attempts at improvement along the way, with several stations replaced by new ones on the Docklands Light Railway network, but there's still plenty of work to be done. In the meantime it provides you with the opportunity to explore one of the most fascinating boroughs the city has to offer, full of reminders of industries that have all but disappeared, and a community of people making the best of the situation they have, living literally in the shadows of the rich world of big business just across the water in and around Canary Wharf.

START: Shadwell (National Rail or Docklands Light Railway)

FINISH: Bow Church (Docklands Light Railway)

TIME: 1 hour, 30 minutes

Shadwell is actually two separate stations, one served by London Overground's East London Line, while the other is on the Docklands Light Railway (DLR). The walk can be started by exiting either one, on to Watney Street. It's a station that's had a complicated history since it opened in 1876 as part of the original East London Line, owned by the East London Railway.

The first station building was located close by on the corner of Cornwall Street, and had its name changed to Shadwell & St George in the East between 1900–1918. It was closed in 1983 and finally succumbed to the bulldozers in 2010. It was replaced by the one used today, at which point the East

Shadwell station building, closed in 1941.

London Line was now part of the London Underground network. This new station was itself closed from 2007-2010 while the line was redeveloped and reopened as part of a new incarnation of the East London Line, now run by London Overground. The DLR station meanwhile opened in 1987.

Turn right on to Martha Street just after the DLR station, keeping the rail viaduct on your left. At the end, turn right under the bridge, and immediately after, on the right side of the road you'll find the remains of another **Shadwell** railway station. This one opened in 1840 as part of the London and Blackwall Railway (L&BR), leased from the Great Eastern Railway (GER). The line ran from Minories in the City to Blackwall, with branches added later that also served a number of stations to Bow and North Greenwich on the Isle of Dogs. The station's name was changed to Shadwell & St George's East in 1900, and it operated for just over a century before finally closing in 1941.

Meagre traces of the station can be seen along Shadwell Place, most of which now appear to be used as commercial premises. There also used to be a covered walkway that allowed passengers to interchange with the other Shadwell station, but almost all signs of this have since disappeared.

Head back under the bridge and continue straight on to what is now Sutton Street, although this isn't signposted. Turn right at the end on to the busy Commercial Road and continue along. The original viaduct that now carries the DLR can be seen by looking down any of the side streets running off to the right. After roughly ten minutes you will reach **Limehouse** DLR and railway station.

It opened under the name Stepney in 1840 as another stop on the L&BR, serving both its main route to Blackwall and the extension to Bow. Most of the platforms were closed in 1926, three years after the name of the station was changed to Stepney East. The station was then used by the London, Tilbury and Southend line, and trains on this route still call at the station today. The station name was changed to Limehouse when the DLR opened its own platforms in the late 1980s.

Walk under the bridge, noting the black arched doorways that likely lead to disused parts of the station. Continue straight, pausing for a second before you reach the next rail bridge to admire the beautiful view to the right of the lock and Limehouse Basin marina, where the Regents Canal meets the Thames, and DLR services run along the viaduct up above.

After crossing the canal a second time further ahead, turn right on to Newell Street, just before the Grade II listed but now almost abandoned Limehouse Town Hall. When you reach the rail bridge, the area on either side is the former location of a different **Limehouse** station, opened in 1840 as another stop on the L&BR. Closure came in 1926, although it

All that is now left of the original Limehouse station.

remained in use for freight until the 1960s. Today the tracks above are used by the DLR, and the location of where the old platforms used to be can easily be spotted on the section between Limehouse and Westferry with blue steel arches over the tracks (these can also be seen from the street).

Retrace your steps back to Commercial Road and continue in the same direction you were headed before. Shortly after passing Nicholas Hawksmoor's St Anne's Limehouse church on the right, turn left on to Burdett Road, catching a quick glance of a great view over Canary Wharf as you do so. After about five minutes, a railway bridge over the road just after a go kart track is the location of **Burdett Road** station. It opened in 1871 as part of the extended L&BR line to Bow, but closed in 1941 after suffering stiff competition from nearby Mile End tube station. Little remains of the station, but there are some traces under the viaduct, now used as commercial premises.

Continue along, passing Mile End Park, before turning left at the busy junction on to Mile End Road. This isn't signposted, but is easy to recognise by the colourful green and yellow bridge that passes over the top. After a few minutes, turn right on to Globe Road, just before Stepney Green tube station.

When you reach the next rail bridge, the area on the right under the viaduct is all that now remains of **Globe Road** station, opened in 1839 on a line originally owned by the Eastern Counties Railway (ECR) that now forms part of the Great Eastern Main Line. Closure came in 1916 but the bricked up entrance can be seen along an alleyway through the original station gates, now leading to a kickboxing gym and a rundown snooker club.

Proceed under the bridge and then turn right on to Roman Road. After about five minutes the road crosses over the canal again, where more views are to be had of Canary Wharf; providing a stark contrast to the impoverished East London estates seen here. Turn right on to Grove Road shortly after, then left on to Antill Road, and right again, this time on to Coborn Road.

The area under the right side of the next bridge is the former location of **Coborn Road** station, opened in 1865 on the same route as Globe Road, and closing in 1946 after losing huge numbers of passengers to various tube stations close by. The original arched doorway that served as the station entrance can still clearly be seen, along with a few other vague traces further along.

Follow Coborn Road to the end, and then turn left on to Mile End Road. The next rail bridge, reached just after passing Bow Road tube station, marks the site of **Bow Road** railway station. It opened in 1876 as the terminus of the L&BR extension, and was originally sited on the right side of the road, but was moved to the left side in 1892, before closing decades

The original arched doorway to the closed Coborn Road station.

Bow Road station building, still standing and now a betting shop.

Brickwork remains of Bow Road platform steps.

later in 1949. Remains of brickwork steps leading to the platforms can easily be seen along Addington Road, and the station building itself still remains intact on the other side of the bridge, currently used as a betting shop.

Continue along until you get to a petrol station on the left side of the road. The car hire company just ahead sits on what used to be **Bow** station, a grand building originally opened in 1850 and rebuilt on a much bigger scale in 1870. It was served by both the GER and the North London Railway, parts of which now form the North London Line. It closed in 1944 and was demolished years later, with nothing but a commemorative plaque on the wall left to suggest it was ever there. Frustratingly, the plaque itself is hidden away in the locked car hire yard. There are however elements of the station still visible at track level, and these can be seen by looking through the fence along the wonderfully named Kitcat Terrace.

Trackside remains of Bow station, now passed through by DLR trains.

Cross over the road to **Bow Church** DLR station, which is the end of the walk. It was opened in 1987, and it's tracks run under the road and through the old Bow station site on the way to Pudding Mill Lane, giving you the chance to get a closer look at the remains seen from Kitcat Terrace.

Bow Church is also a short walk from Bow Road tube station on the Hammersmith & City and District lines. It's also only two short stops away from Stratford, where interchange is available with various rail services and the Central and Jubilee lines.

TRAIN JOURNEYS

The train rides that follow give you the chance to see platforms and other trackside remains of many stations featured in the walks. You'll have to be quick to see some sites, but visual clues have been provided that give you a rough idea of when to look.

A London one day Travelcard should allow you to easily travel each journey, and all stations fall inside TfL's Oyster card zones, though the use of an Oyster card as a Travelcard is not recommended as it is easy to be overcharged.

The journey time totals are approximate, based on a typical run with no delays.

Journey 1

Start: West Hampstead Thameslink (First Capital Connect)
Finish: Herne Hill (Southeastern). **Duration:** 32 minutes

Start by catching a First Capital Connect Thameslink train headed for Sutton. Look out of the right side of the train just after pulling out of West Hampstead Thameslink and you'll see the overgrown remains of what appears to be disused track and sidings. Then, just before the train disappears into the Belsize Tunnels, you'll see an overgrown area of weeds and brick. This is the remains of the platforms of **Finchley Road** station (covered in Walk 3).

After emerging from the long tunnel, the open section of cutting is the former location of the platforms at **Haverstock Hill** station, including fragments of brickwork and concrete that can be seen from both sides of the train.

Just after the train passes through Kentish Town station, the open area just before the train enters the Camden Road Tunnels marks where the **Camden Road** station platforms used to be (included in the same walk as Finchley Road above). No traces remain, although a large space between the current tracks hints that something used to be there.

After stopping at St Pancras International station, the train continues through another section of tunnel as it passes beneath the rest of the station and Kings Cross. A few minutes later, it passes through the disused **Kings Cross Thameslink** platforms, still largely intact and recognisable by the many boarded-up doorways and 'Do Not Alight Here' signs. The station is included in Walk 2.

The train then stops at Farringdon, before entering the Snow Hill Tunnel immediately afterwards. Mid-way through the tunnel, the derelict remains of the old **Snow Hill** station platforms can be seen through the windows on either side of the train (included in Walk 1). It emerges from the tunnel at City Thameslink station, which itself is built on the former site of **Holborn Viaduct** station (covered in the same walk as Snow Hill).

The route then crosses the Thames via Blackfriars station, and just after it reaches the other side, a small section of wider trackside space seen through the right windows is all that now remains of the **Blackfriars Bridge** station platforms, including a few traces of old brickwork. The station itself is listed in the same walk as Snow Hill and Holborn Viaduct mentioned above.

Although it's hard to see, the arched-steel bridge passed through just before the train reaches Elephant & Castle station is where the platforms of **Borough Road** station once stood, and the train then passes through the long-gone **Walworth Road** platforms a few minutes later. Seconds after, the train then travels past the scant remains of **Camberwell** station, including a wider, overgrown section of trackside between the centre two tracks with the top of the old white station building also visible at the point where the route passes a bus depot. A short while later the train arrives at **Loughborough Junction** station, where a set of abandoned and derelict platforms can easily be seen through the left windows. Note that Borough Road, Walworth Road, Camberwell and Loughborough Junction are all included in Walk 7.

The journey ends when the train arrives at **Herne Hill**. Although the station now has four platforms, there used to be five, and the bricked-up part of the station that gave access to the old platform can be seen. A recently built siding occupies the site of the old fifth platform.

Journey 2

Start: Clapham Junction (London Overground). **Finish:** Euston (National Rail, Northern and Victoria lines). **Duration:** 45 minutes (includes interchange time at Willesden Junction)

Abandoned platform 1 at Clapham Junction station.

Enter **Clapham Junction** station and find a London Overground train headed for Willesden Junction from platform 2. But just before boarding, look at the overgrown area adjacent to the platform and you'll see the now-disused platform 1.

After the train passes Imperial Wharf station, an area between two bridges close to Chelsea's Stamford Bridge stadium marks the former site of **Chelsea & Fulham** station, recognisable by overgrown traces of the old platforms on either side of the train. Shortly after, the train then stops at **West Brompton**, where a few elements of the old station layout can just about still be seen. West Brompton and Chelsea & Fulham stations are both included in Walk 4.

Exit the train at Willesden Junction and change on to the London Overground service to Euston. Just after the train leaves **Kilburn High Road** station, the overgrown trackside area, seen through the right, hints at the other two platforms that have long since been removed. A few minutes later the train arrives at **South Hampstead**, where more significant elements of its own closed two platforms can be seen along the right. This and Kilburn High Road stations are explored in more detail in Walk 3.

Immediately after South Hampstead, the train disappears into one of the Primrose Hill Tunnel portals, emerging on the other side in a wide cutting. The area on the left just after the next bridge is the former location of **Primrose Hill** station, and its abandoned brickwork and decaying platforms can easily be seen, as can the **Roundhouse** just after. The tunnel, station and Roundhouse are all included in the same Camden walk mentioned above.

The journey ends when the train arrives at **Euston**. The station has its own disused parts at street level, all of which are included in Walk 2.

Journey 3

Start: Highbury & Islington (London Overground). **Finish:** Whitechapel (District, Hammersmith & City lines). **Duration:** 13 minutes

Take a London Overground train from Highbury & Islington, headed for Crystal Palace, New Cross or West Croydon (see the *More Things to See* section for a look at Highbury & Islington's own disused station building). When the train leaves Dalston Junction station, the track begins to run high above the streets on a stretch of the Kingsland Viaduct, passing through the remains of the old platforms of **Shoreditch** railway station, until disappearing into a huge concrete structure as it reaches Shoreditch High Street.

The station is built on an extensive part of the former **Bishopsgate**, **Bishopsgate Low Level** and **Bishopsgate Goods Yard** sites, derelict and overgrown parts of which can easily be seen down below on the right side of the train after it leaves Shoreditch High Street. Shortly after, the train then passes the old **Shoreditch** Underground station building on the right, and the decaying remains of **Spitalfields Goods Yard** on the left. All of the above stations and sites are included in Walk 5. The journey ends when you arrive at Whitechapel.

Journey 4

Start: Victoria (Southeastern). **Finish:** Lewisham (National Rail, DLR). **Duration:** 21 minutes

Board a Southeastern train at Victoria heading for Dartford (note that this service runs at certain times of day only, and not on Sundays), and look out of the left window. Just before the track crosses over the River Thames, the old **Grosvenor**

Road station building can be seen alongside the road, followed shortly after by views from the bridge towards Battersea Power Station and the former site of **Pimlico/ Battersea Wharf** stations. All three stations are covered in more detail in Walk 6.

The train then heads south, passing through the almost-completely disappeared remains of **East Brixton** station (Walk 7) a few minutes before stopping at Denmark Hill. Just after stopping at **Nunhead,** traces of the original station site can be seen on both sides, before then passing through the remains of **Brockley Lane** station on a stretch of viaduct directly above the London Bridge to Brighton main line. The route then runs along a cutting, part of which includes the trackside remains of **Lewisham Road** station, with still-intact brick work visible on the right side just after the train emerges from a bridge. Nunhead, Brockley Lane and Lewisham Road are all covered in Walk 8. The journey ends a few minutes later when you reach Lewisham.

Journey 5

Start: London Bridge (Southeastern). **Finish:** Deptford (National Rail) and Deptford Bridge Docklands Light Railway (DLR). **Duration:** 6 minutes

This short journey starts at London Bridge and gives you the chance to travel along vast sections of the **London Bridge – Greenwich Railway Viaduct**. The elevated tracks pass through numerous road bridges along the way, two of which include the former platforms of both **Spa Road** and **Southwark Park** stations, although their scant remains are hard to spot. The viaduct and both former stations are included in Walk 7. The journey ends when you reach Deptford a few minutes later.

TUBE JOURNEYS

The following Underground rides take you through many of the stations included in the 12 walks, with a few additional extras. Much of what can be seen goes by at blink-and-you'll-miss-it speed, so you better be ready. You are literally gazing out of the window into a pitch black tunnel for the most part, lit only by the glow of the train itself. For this reason, the best way to see things is to keep your face as close to the window as possible, using your hands to block out the lights from the carriage. Again, journey time totals are approximate, based on a typical run with no delays.

Journey 1

Start: Gloucester Road (Circle/District and Piccadilly lines).
Finish: Arsenal (Piccadilly). **Duration:** 30 minutes

Start at **Gloucester Road** station and head for the Circle/District line platforms. Opposite platform 3 you'll find a disused platform, with its brickwork arches still intact and often used for art installations. Now board any eastbound District or Circle line train. Get off at the next stop, **South Kensington**, which also has its own disused platforms, the eastbound one visible on the opposite side of the tracks from platform 2 and the westbound one opposite platform 1.

Follow signs to the Piccadilly line platforms and get on an eastbound train to Cockfosters. Peer out of the windows on the right side of the train between South Kensington and Knightsbridge, and you'll notice that the colour of the tunnel wall changes for a few seconds from dark-metal to reddish-brick. This marks the location of the former **Brompton Road** platforms, hidden from passing trains after the station's closure in 1934.

A similar underground brickwork section can be seen between Hyde Park Corner and Green Park, this time hiding the existence of **Down Street** station, closed in 1932. When the train leaves Holborn, look out of the right side immediately after and you should be able to get a quick glimpse of an old set of tracks running off into a disused tunnel. This is where trains used to run to **Aldwych** station via a short branch line, before it was closed in 1994. Brompton Road and Down Street stations are covered in detail in Walk 4. Aldwych meanwhile is covered in Walk 1.

Disused eastbound platform at South Kensington. The four tracks that existed here until the 1960s enabled fast trains to operate on the District line between Sloane Square and Earl's Court.

During the long gap between Kings Cross St Pancras and Caledonian Road stations, look out of the right side and about halfway through you can clearly see the remains of **York Road** station. Closed in 1932, it is easily recognisable as an open area of wider tunnel with various dark passages, although the platforms themselves are long gone. The station building appears in Walk 2.

The journey ends when you reach **Arsenal**, where you'll notice that the tiling along the wall lists the station as being called Gillespie Road. This was its original name on opening in 1906, changed later to Arsenal (Highbury Hill) when it became the closest station to the football club's former stadium at Highbury. The 'Highbury Hill' suffix was then dropped in the early 1960s.

Original name tiling at Arsenal station.

Journey 2

Start: Finchley Road (Metropolitan line). **Finish:** Liverpool Street (Central, Metropolitan, Circle and Hammersmith & City lines). **Duration:** 21 minutes

Begin at **Finchley Road** and get on a southbound Metropolitan line train to Aldgate (not one that terminates at Baker Street). Look out into the darkness on the right side of the train and after a short while you'll see a stretch of wider tunnel, with what appears to be a metal fire escape staircase and other equipment. These are the abandoned **Swiss Cottage** platforms, closed in 1940 when the station was resited.

Soon after, the train passes through gaps in the tunnel that mark the site of disused **Marlborough Road** station, also closed in 1940. Although most of the actual concrete platforms have been removed, travelling during daylight hours lets you easily see various arched doorways and passages on either side of the train, along with metal steps that now act as a fire exit via the still-intact station building above. Both former stations are included in Walk 3.

Not long after, another similar site can be seen through the right side just before the train exits the tunnel for a short stretch on its approach to Baker Street. Now used as a fire exit and housing for ventilation equipment, it's actually the remains of **Lords** station, which closed at the same time as Swiss Cottage and Marlborough Road. Nothing remains of the station building above except for the door from the fire escape, which can be seen behind the Danibus hotel on Lodge Street, close to Lord's cricket ground.

A minute or so after leaving Kings Cross St Pancras station; the train briefly emerges out of the tunnel, and on the right side can be seen the one remaining platform of the original **Kings Cross Underground** station, still easily recognisable as a platform despite being derelict and used for storage. The

Disused platforms at Barbican station, with abandoned tunnels to Smithfield market.

wall seen through the left side hides **Kings Cross Thameslink** station, itself also now disused. Both stations are covered in Walk 2. Step off the train when it reaches **Barbican**, opened in 1865 under the name Aldersgate Street. Its disused platforms 3 and 4 can be seen, taken out of service when Thameslink trains stopped running to Moorgate in 2009. There is also a disused but well-preserved signal box at one end of the platforms, to the left of which can be seen fenced-off tunnels that formerly served nearby Smithfield Market.

Get back on to the next eastbound train, and then jump off again when it reaches **Moorgate**. As with Barbican, the station includes its own set of platforms that have been disused since 2009, this time numbers 5 and 6, still intact and easy to see alongside the tube line platforms. Wait for the next eastbound train and get back on. Exit the train again at the next stop, **Liverpool Street**, which also has a disused bay platform that can still partially be seen from one end of the current platforms. This is where the journey ends.

Journey 3

Start: Stockwell (Northern and Victoria lines). **Finish:** Golders Green (Option 1) or Kentish Town (Northern line) (Option 2). **Duration:** 34 or 27 minutes respectively.

Begin at **Stockwell**, which was resited to its present location in the 1920s. The original platforms can still be seen from one end of the Northern line platforms, recognisable as a wider area just after the end of the current platforms, usually well lit and with some original tile work still visible. Stockwell station and its deep-level shelters are included in Walk 6. Now get on board the next northbound Bank-branch Northern line train.

Look out of the left side of the window just after the train leaves Borough station, and you should be able to see a dark and disused tunnel running away from the main tracks. This leads to the abandoned **King William Street** station, closed in 1900 and covered in Walk 1.

In the long gap between Old Street and Angel stations, the forgotten remains of **City Road** station can be seen, easy to spot as a stretch of wider tunnel, with grimy white tiling and dark passages visible, although the actual platforms have been taken away. It closed in 1922 and is covered in Walk 5.

At **Camden Town** you have two options. Option 1 is an Edgware-branch train. Notice as you pass through **Hampstead** station that the tiling along the walls lists the station as being Heath Street – its originally proposed name before this was decided against just before opening in 1907.

Between Hampstead and Golders Green station, look out of the right side of the train and you'll notice a wider section of open tunnel, now used for storage. This marks the location of **North End**; a never-completed station that was abandoned in 1906 when it was predicted that it would never be a financial success. Also known by its nickname **Bull & Bush**, it would have been the deepest station on the Underground network. Some work on the street-level building was completed, now converted into an anonymous looking fire escape that can be seen on Hampstead Way, just off North End Road. This part of the journey ends when you reach Golders Green.

Option 2 is a High Barnet or Mill Hill East train. Soon after leaving Camden Town, the remains of the old platform area of **South Kentish Town** station can easily be seen on both sides of the train, recognisable as a wider stretch of tunnel with various dark passages (the station building is included in Walk 3). This part of the journey ends when the train arrives at Kentish Town.

Journey 4

Start: Tottenham Court Road (Central and Northern lines). **Finish:** Whitechapel (District, Hammersmith & City lines, London Overground). **Duration:** 21 minutes (includes interchange time at Bank)

Take an eastbound Central line train from Tottenham Court Road and immediately look out of the windows on the right hand side. After around half a minute, you'll see the tunnel open out to a wider size, and another set of tracks veering off to the right. Just after this, another wider section of tunnel marks the abandoned platforms of **British Museum** station, closed in 1933. The platforms themselves have been removed, but white tiling and various dark doorways and passages can be seen as the train passes through. Although demolished, the former location of the station building is given in Walk 1.

The train arrives at **Holborn** shortly after, where various locked doors can be seen alongside several entrances to the eastbound Piccadilly line platforms. These hide the former passageways to two disused platforms; one of which, platform 6, was taken out of service in 1917 and later converted into an air raid shelter. The other, platform 5, was used for trains on the short branch line to **Aldwych** station (see Walk 1 for more), which was closed in 1994. It is however still used as a test platform for new innovations and improvements.

Continue the journey until you reach Bank station. Leave the Central line train here and follow signs for the Circle and District line platforms. After a long walk through almost the entire station, you will finally emerge at the platforms, but in fact will now be inside Monument station (the two stations are connected by passageways and escalators).

Step on to an eastbound District line train headed for Upminster. Between Monument and the next stop at Tower Hill, looking out through either side of the train allows you to see traces of **Mark Lane** station, including a staircase which is sometimes lit. It closed in 1967, and is covered in Walk 1.

Before the train arrives at **Aldgate East**, it's just about possible to make out a wider area where the original station's platforms sat before being resited in 1938, followed shortly after passing the current station by the remains of a former connection to the East London line and **St Mary's** station, closed as a result of the new Aldgate East site. Both stations are included in Walk 5. The journey ends soon after when the train arrives at Whitechapel.

MORE THINGS TO SEE

London is a big place, which makes the task of including everything almost impossible. What follows is a list of some other stations and sites, none of which fit logically into any of the walking routes but are still worth finding.

Belsize Park Deep Level Shelter
Belsize Park is one of the eight Underground stations that had an extra tunnel built under their main platforms for use in World War II (see Walk 1, Walk 2 and Walk 6 for more on the rest of the deep level shelters). The southern entrance to the shelter can easily be spotted as the rounded white structure further down Haverstock Hill from the tube station entrance, on the corner of Downside Crescent. The northern entrance is located further uphill from the tube station, hidden down a path that runs between a coffee shop and house number 212.

St Ann's Road Station
Opened in 1882 by the Tottenham & Hampstead Junction Railway, St Ann's Road struggled to attract passengers and closed its doors in 1942. The small station building is still standing as a newsagent, and can be seen on Seven Sisters Road, close to the junction with St Ann's Road.

Necropolis Railway Station
Perhaps the quirkiest abandoned railway station in London is located at 121 Westminster Bridge Road. Although now used for commercial purposes, the building is the former home of the London Necropolis Railway station. The railway was used to transport bodies by train to Brookwood Cemetery in Surrey. The building seen today is actually a replacement to an original opened in 1899 that had to be demolished to make room for plans to expand nearby Waterloo station. The new site was opened in 1902 but closed after damage sustained during World War II.

What was once Necropolis station, from where bodies were transported to a cemetery in Surrey.

23/24 Leinster Gardens

Not strictly abandoned but still a great hidden gem, the two houses at this address near Bayswater have something a little strange about them. When engineers were building what today is the Circle line, they needed to provide a gap in the tunnelling for steam from passing trains to disperse, and it meant that two houses on this street needed to be demolished. But the fact that the houses were part of an affluent terrace meant that the idea didn't go down too well.

Left Fake building frontage at 23–24 Leinster Gardens, W2.

Above Rear of the fake frontage at Leinster Gardens. Trains still run below today.

So, after demolishing the two houses, they had to maintain the terrace frontages by providing a fake facade. Closer inspection reveals that the windows of the houses are actually painted on the walls, and that the doors have no letter boxes. Circle and District line trains run below, recognisable as a small open section of tunnel between Bayswater and Paddington.

Abandoned Highbury & Islington Station Building

A disused entrance hall at Highbury & Islington tube and train station can clearly be seen on the opposite side of Holloway Road to the current entrance. It's one of two original station buildings, opened by the Great Northern & City Railway (GN&CR) in 1904. The installation of escalators in the 1960s meant that the station had to be remodelled and the old entrance was replaced by the one used today. The Holloway Road side was given a mismatched paint job in 2006, but better preserved parts of the building, including additional entrances, can be seen by turning off the main road on to Highbury Place and then turning left on to Highbury Crescent.

Highbury & Islington station building on Holloway Road, taken out of service in the 1960s.

Highgate Road Stations

Highgate Road High and Low level stations were opened by the Tottenham & Hampstead Junction Railway in 1868 and 1900 respectively. The High level closed in 1915, followed by the Low level station three years later in 1918. Most of the station buildings still remain intact however, and can be seen under a rail bridge along Highgate Road in North London, close to the corner of Wesleyan Place.

Osterley Park & Spring Grove Station

The station was opened in 1883 by the Metropolitan District Railway on a branch line that ran to Hounslow. By the early 1930s however, the Underground Group opened a new station close by at Osterley, rendering the original one redundant. The building remains intact as a shop, and can be found on Thornbury Road, close to the entrance to Osterley Park itself on Jersey Road. If you travel there by Piccadilly line through Hammersmith, look out for a former London & South Western Railway viaduct on the right of the train just after leaving the tunnel west of Hammersmith station. It provided a connection here from the Hammersmith & City line.

Old Station Names

One of the Bakerloo line platforms at **Marylebone** station includes tiling on the wall that shows the station as being named Great Central. That was its name on opening in 1907, but it was changed to its current name in 1917. A similar situation can be seen at **Warren Street**, where the Northern line platform tiling displays its original 1907 name of Euston Road. Arsenal and Hampstead tube stations also have old names displayed in their tile work, and these are included in the tube journeys from Gloucester Road to Arsenal and Stockwell to Golders Green.

There are other abandoned tube and rail buildings elsewhere around the city and along its miles of track, plus various other sites where old stations have disappeared without a trace. But you'll have to discover those for yourself. Happy hunting.

References and Further Reading

Books

Bayman, B, *Underground Official Handbook*.
   Capital Transport, 2008
Connor, J.E, *London's Disused Stations: Volume Two to
   Seven*. Connor & Butler, 2000–2009.
Connor, J.E, *London's Disused Underground Stations*.
   Capital Transport, 2006
Emmerson, A, *The London Underground*. Shire Library, 2010
Harris, C.M, *What's In a Name*. Capital History, 2008
Price, J, *Postman's Park: G.F. Watts's Memorial to Heroic Self
   Sacrifice*. Watts Gallery, 2008
Smith, S, *Underground London: Travels Beneath The City
   Streets*. Abacus, 2004
Talling, P, *Derelict London*. Random House Books, 2008
Welbourn, N, *Lost Lines London*. Ian Allan, 2008

Websites

http://www.abandonedstations.org.uk/
http://www.derelictlondon.com/
http://www.disused-stations.org.uk/
http://www.ltmcollection.org/photos/
http://londonrailways.net/
http://www.mailrail.co.uk/
http://www.subbrit.org.uk/
http://underground-history.co.uk/
http://en.wikipedia.org/
http://www.28dayslater.co.uk/forums/

INDEX